Tales of Mogadiscio

Iris Kapil

Light Messages
www.lightmessages.com

In memory of my husband.

With special thanks to Gerry Lynch and Shirley Wiegand without whose help I could not have completed this work.

CONTENTS

FOREWORD

Mogadiscio in the 1960s seemed, then as now, a city at the end of the earth. Yet, in those years it was a lovely city with a remarkable architecture, peaceful and well-governed. I lived there for two years, a young mother caring for her family but deeply engaged, as well, in the fascinating world around me. I would remember Mogadiscio, vividly, and tell my friends stories about its people and places. Finally, when I at last had time to write the stories, Somalia had changed, totally and fundamentally. Mogadiscio is in shambles, warfare never ceases and government exists in name only.

I needed to rethink my memories. I felt I should take on an enlarged purpose: not only to present scenes from the Mogadiscio I knew but also to arrive at an understanding, however limited, of what has befallen it and Somalia in the years after I left. I caught up with Somalia's recent history, recalled and examined my observations and added essays, drawing on my peculiar background as an anthropologist with an M.B.A. and on the wisdom my husband had gained during his years as an international civil servant.

Somalia's more recent history would not have been predicted during the 1960s, in that first decade after independence; everyone my husband and I knew and the people with whom we talked felt optimistic about its future. During the 1950s Somali leaders had been prepared, under a United Nations mandate, for their roles in the new government and they impressed us all with their political skills. Unlike other African states, Somalia was relatively homogeneous in language and identity; it was generally believed that progress would not be thwarted by tribal and ethnic differences. Foreign aid and expertise for Somalia were more than generous and we could see considerable benefit resulting from it.

Then in 1969, the Somali army, well equipped by the Russians, staged a coup d'état, introducing Soviet-style "scientific socialism" for a brief period of peace that was followed by war of clan against clan. In 1991, the dictator fled Mogadiscio, leaving behind a failed state that has not been reconstituted. Death and violence reigned. Innumerable Somalis fled or became internal refugees, destitute, hungry, depending on foreign aid for sustenance.

By the summer of 2011, the most severe drought in 60 years had devastated the Horn of Africa, and as I write this, Somalis are suffering from famine in what the United Nations calls the world's worst humanitarian disaster. I cannot bring myself to write about Somalia in this dreadful time but must comment that before the drought I had read a number of studies showing the resilience of the people, showing that social order and the economy can be rebuilt. Despite the Islamic and warlord militiamen who continually prey upon them, Somalis in the south had continued farming, raising livestock, carrying on trade and sustaining their towns. Local governing was taking root. Already, in the north, in two regions, Somaliland and Puntland, government and civil society have been organized and continue to function. People live in peace, protected from severe food and water shortages. Towns are growing in size and complexity.

In Mogadiscio life continues, if chaotically. The city grows and spreads into the countryside, well beyond the boundaries of the 1960s Mogadiscio I knew. That Mogadiscio has been destroyed, its people killed or driven into exile. Few, if any, traces of Mogadiscio's past remain. Only in photographs will future generations of Somalis see their first capital city's landscape of gardens and public spaces and its delightful architecture – an array of Benadir, Arabian and Italian style residences and places of religion, government, commerce and leisure that stood at the oceanfront and along the streets inland from the two harbors. Other cities of the East Africa coast, particularly Mombasa and Zanzibar, guarding their heritage and with tourism in mind, have preserved their ancient and colonial period buildings in a defined Historic District. No such District is as attractive as Mogadiscio's could have been. I grieve for the people and all that has been lost.

2

MRS. MILLER IN MOGADISCIO

I once believed, long ago, that when I grew old I would become another Mrs. Miller. Now I have passed the age she was then and the dream has not been realized. Occasionally an image of her small, solid figure, reassuringly calm, rises into my consciousness and I find myself reflecting on the time when she and I shared a space on this earth. I think of her fine work and wonder if, after all, it was worth the effort. I wonder if she invested too much of herself, to no avail, in a beguiling city and countryside that was destined to become a pandemonium, an abode for demons.

Ours was the Cold War era, a time when Western democracies and the Soviet Union competed for influence in poor but strategically located Third World countries. Superpowers poured money and personnel into areas marginal to their economic interests, ostensibly to give aid for economic development but primarily to maintain a presence and keep the other side out. Then the Berlin Wall fell and the very idea of a Third World between First and Second Worlds lost all meaning. The great powers withdrew, leaving behind countries that were still poor and poorly governed, left on their own with burgeoning populations, rising expectations and an abundant supply of arms.

For Mrs. Miller and me the Third World country was Somalia.

I met Mrs. Miller in 1963 at a cocktail party in Mogadiscio, a reception for diplomats, dignitaries and the few Americans who, like my husband and me, were in Somalia for research or, like Mrs. Miller, for her own idiosyncratic reason. The reception was held in an elegant, beautifully furnished official residence surrounded by well-tended gardens. An ocean breeze drifted in through French doors. From a phonograph somewhere floated the softly muted sound of jazz piano. A uniformed serving staff moved among us, filling our glasses with the finest of wines or handing us pleasantly chilled drinks, offering us canapés artfully crafted from imported foods.

Outside the residence's compound walls lay a scrub landscape that in the best of times barely yields a living to its people and periodically decimates them with drought or flood. A Somali once described man as a handful of dust caught in a sandstorm.

Being newly arrived and curious, and this my first social affair in Somalia, I watched from the sidelines. The diplomats and dignitaries circulated. They appeared relaxed and casual, but I sensed they were working, gathering information and assessing one another. The wives clustered together, chatting. They were chic, fashionably tanned, fashionably dressed. I overheard snatches of conversation about children and servants and where to go in Europe on vacation. At such affairs, diplomats' wives necessarily kept to generalities. I could imagine their situation -- never offend anyone, never say or do anything controversial, stay within the boundaries defined for an embassy wife.

Mrs. Miller was standing alone, serenely observing the scene around us. Her detached manner and benign expression intrigued me. She looked to be in her middle 60s, straight and solidly built. Her thick, gray streaked black hair, braided and wrapped around her head, and strong, comely features reminded me of Italian immigrant women I had known as a child. She wore a sun-faded cotton frock, sensible shoes and held at her side a sensible broad-rimmed hat. I worked my way across the room to where she stood and offered something, I forget what, to strike up a conversation. She smiled warmly at me but said that she was about to leave. She explained briefly that people were waiting for her, and she had many things to do before the morning.

Mrs. Miller became a part of my life in Mogadiscio although I never met her again and saw her only occasionally, at a distance. During my entire time in the city, wherever I turned, she had been there or was somewhere nearby.

My husband, Raj, and I and our two small children lived in Mogadiscio "on the economy"; we were on a one-year research grant, unaffiliated, unsupported by any organization. We rented a house in a neighborhood of middle-level United Nations personnel and their families, each house set in a small compound filled with trees and shrubs, surrounded by a high white wall topped with glass shards or sharp wire and entered through a single wrought iron gate at the road. Our house was a plain box of cinder block walls, plastered and white-washed, set on a cement slab, divided into two bedrooms and a bathroom, equipped with electric lighting and piped-in brackish water. The roof, made of tin sheeting, extended about ten feet beyond the white walls and rested on outer walls of louvered wood panels painted a dark green. Our sitting and dining area was a space in the front of the house, between the white and the green walls. Mostly we sat outside under the bougainvillea arbor. In the bathroom were a sink and a toilet and a showerhead suspended from a ceiling pipe situated over a drain in the cement floor. The furniture - - beds, cotton filled mattresses, shelving, table, chairs -- had been made locally and was as plain as furniture can be. The kitchen, at the back of the house, was another between-the-walls room. It held a sink, a stove fueled by a half-sized propane gas tank, a tiny electric refrigerator and a small wall cupboard. We kept dry foods in a cabinet with doors made of iron mesh as protection against rodents, enormous winged beetles, insects of every imaginable variety. Feral cats and the occasional monkey regularly came over the outside wall, through a gap under the roof, so one had constantly to watch for them. We did laundry in the back garden, with the brackish water flowing from a spigot into a large cement basin. Outside the kitchen stood a zinc barrel for our drinking water, which we bought from a rattley old truck that used at least half the water in its tank to keep the rusted-out radiator full.

Wherever it went, the truck left a wet line on the dusty road to mark its passing.

On our first day in residence a tall, matriarchal woman, Asha, from a nearby Somali neighborhood came to inform us that we needed a boyessa to sweep and clean and take care of us, so we hired her, and she brought Ahmed as our guard. They spoke Italian, the language of their former colonial masters, so I learned to communicate in basic Italian and a fluent vocabulary of gestures. Men from a local Indian merchant community, English speaking, befriended Raj and accepted me despite my being American rather than Indian. They showed us how to shop and the women taught me how to cook with food available in the markets. Our two children were accepted into a primary school maintained by the American Embassy for their families. Local medical care was adequate and in an emergency we could have turned to our Embassy for help.

Mrs. Miller and I and my family were living in a unique small world. Mogadiscio had retained the accoutrements of an Italian colonial town and was thoroughly charming as such: Italian and Arabian architecture; tree-lined streets, paved and with sidewalks; parks and gardens, artfully designed, still being tended with care. A well functioning municipal system provided a full complement of facilities for residents and outsiders: banks, shops, restaurants, cafés, hotels, a soccer field and a tennis court. A diesel-fueled power station generated electricity for streetlights on the main roads, for public buildings and for the houses of people, mostly foreigners, who could afford it. For public health there were sewage and drainage systems and the municipal pumping of brackish water to residences. Household trash was collected and disposed of, probably at the oceanfront to be washed out by the tide. Telephone lines in the downtown ran to official establishments and to some of the homes; it never occurred to us that we needed a telephone. Several petrol stations served the relatively light automobile traffic, including

Raj's tiny Fiat 600. Police officers directed traffic. Realistically, they could not protect large residences full of imported goodies from the constant threat of theft, so nearly all foreigners hired a guard or two for the house and compound. Ahmed saw to the security of our possessions; he and his friends kept us company during the day and he slept soundly in our compound at night. We were never robbed. Police presence in the city was light; streets were safe and generally peaceful.

Mogadiscio's population grew in numbers and variety. A multitude of foreign experts of many nationalities, most accompanied by their families, had been brought to Mogadiscio by the United Nations to shape and set into place the various Ministries in Somalia's new government. Embassies were established. They added to the texture of the city with their development programs and the facilities they built to maintain their vehicles and equipment. Their personnel lived in large houses inside compound walls and relaxed in their Embassy's clubhouse that sat in the long, neat row of clubhouses along the beach. The emerging Somali elite, composed of senators, civil servants and a new class of businessmen had moved into the homes of departing Italian families or built modern houses for themselves. Pastoral nomads and village farmers were coming into Mogadiscio and settling on the periphery in small wattle and daub (stick and mud plaster) houses they constructed. We once watched several individuals in from the bush walk past our compound to Asha's neighborhood, their belongings carried on the back of a camel that haughtily ambled along with them.

Raj and I soon made friends among the foreign experts and their families and among the Somalis, many of whom we met through his research. We took the children to the American clubhouse so they could play in the sand and water while we watched over them from the clubhouse porch. The Soviet Union clubhouse was near the American's, but for reasons one can only imagine, we had no contact with one another.

We often met friends at the U.N. clubhouse and partied in one of the few clubhouses owned by a Somali. I spent whatever time I could find outside family and social responsibilities in a *quartier* of Mogadiscio unknown to most foreigners and even to many Somalis. It was the original Mogadiscio, a thousand year old coastal city of narrow, unpaved streets; residences and shops in two- and three-story and a few four-story flat-roofed, whitewashed buildings; small mosques and Somalia's central mosque. Men wore their traditional dress and many women were veiled in public. Somalis called the old city Hamar Wein. By the 1960s, Hamar Wein had become dilapidated but livable and intact as a community.

I moved among people and in places other expatriates and the local elite did not often see. Except for Mrs. Miller. She not only saw; she acted.

Somali friends told me that Mrs. Miller had been a schoolteacher in California. When she retired on a small pension, and after her husband died, it would seem that she decided to follow her calling elsewhere, in another country. I suspect she spoke Italian, for she sought out former Italian colonies. She sailed first to Libya and spent a while in Tripoli, as if trying it out, then boarded a ship headed east and landed in Mogadiscio, a town that suited her just fine, as it did me.

My image of Mrs. Miller's house comes from my children's description of it. They had talked me into having Ahmed walk them after school to Mrs. Miller's house. They told me that Mrs. Miller had electricity and water but no refrigerator; her sitting room was furnished with only a table and a few chairs; her windows were not screened, so she used a mosquito net over her bed. I asked the children why they visited her. She had been at their school one day and they had talked with her and she said they could come to see her. I asked what they did at her house. Nothing. They simply liked being with her.

Mrs. Miller created projects that kept her busier than most of the experts working in various Embassy-operated official development programs. She used her small house as a language classroom. A command of English was a valuable asset for a Somali in finding a good job and improving his or her station in life. Many times when I was walking about in Mogadiscio a young man would approach me and speak to me in English, as if testing himself, finding out if a foreigner would actually understand and respond. When I sat among Somalis in the gallery of the National Assembly watching senators on the floor below, young men and boys in their late teens came and sat beside me, with no motive other than to carry on a conversation in their newly acquired language. One young man in particular conspicuously held a little red book, "The Thoughts of Mao" for me to see, defiantly announcing his political ideology to this American woman. When I asked him and the others, persons who obviously were not of means and unlikely able to afford tutoring, where they had learned English, invariably they answered, "Mrs. Miller."

Mrs. Miller acquired a typewriter and taught typing. When someone needed a letter composed in proper English, she was there as super secretary. She supported good causes by badgering the local Italian language newspaper, Corriere della Somalia, with well-reasoned and fully documented statements on important public issues. When she discovered a compound where abandoned blind children, about twenty of them, were barely coping, she informed several Embassy wives and they organized a project to take food and clothing to the children. Mrs. Miller learned Braille and, because the Somali language at that time had no official script, she taught the children English and Braille in English. She somehow found money, possibly from her own modest income, to buy Braille watches, one for each child.

In the 1960s, the path that Mrs. Miller had taken, a teacher moving to a distant land where people needed her and would welcome her, did not seem to me in any way strange or dangerous. She was acting on her values and enjoying an adventure. In Somalia, I never feared for my safety and, evidently, neither did she. I assumed, correctly, as surely did she, that as long as I behaved courteously and was of good will all would go well for me. No one questioned Mrs. Miller's motives or mine as she and I worked with and for Somalis.

Raj and I and the children lived in Mogadiscio for not quite two years, moving back and forth between teaching in our university and doing research in Somalia. One of my last memories of Mogadiscio was of the evening before our final flight from the airport to Nairobi, to Rome and back to America, in June 1967. A Somali police official had invited us to his home for an evening with friends. As we drove through the gate of his compound a young police guard suddenly, abruptly lowered the barrel of a rifle into my face. Why he did this we did not know; we were hardly a threat to him or the police official.

This was my personal reminder of Somalia's recently made small arms agreement with the Soviet Union. It was the beginning of every man and boy having access to weapons they did not understand. I have a Somali bow and quiver of arrows we brought home with us, mostly because I found the bow, with its elongated curves, such a lovely object. The wood looks layered, as if the darker inside were cut from heartwood. The bow is tight and hard to pull; a boy would need training and practice to master this weapon. In Mogadiscio, in an open area near the Italian cemetery, older men gathered to practice archery, to retain their skill and artistry, when at a time soon to come any boy could casually pick up a machine gun and instantly, effortlessly kill or destroy whatever happened to be in his way.

In 1968, Raj and I learned from a friend that Mrs. Miller had left Mogadiscio and, presumably, returned home. An article in the English language *Somali News* told of the large number of Somalis, a few Americans and people of other nationalities she had befriended crowded the airport to honor her and bid her farewell. Men spoke warmly of her that day in the bars and cafes.

In 1969, a faction from within the army staged a coup d'etat against the elected government. A general, Siad Barre, took total command, and in an attempt to modernize Somalia, installed a government modeled on the Russian state. The Soviets financed a period of reform and growth for Mogadiscio and the southern region until 1977. In that year the Somali army crossed the border into an area of Ethiopia, the Ogaden, to protect the rights of indigenous Somali pastoralists. In Ethiopia, a new regime had overthrown Emperor Haile Selassie and declared itself communist, leading the Soviet Union to change sides, from Somalia to Ethiopia. Long and destructive military engagements followed, with many lives lost. In 1980, the U.S. government re-engaged with the Somali government.

Somalia became a miserably governed nation. In 1991, militia forces came together, ousted the dictator, then turned to fighting one another. The savagery increased as gangs of street boys, illiterate, many homeless, joined the fracas to loot, plunder, pillage and casually kill anyone who got in their way. The possibility for public order would have come from the new Somali middle-class, people who were educated and accustomed to a modern mode of living, but they felt compelled to flee, first to Kenya and Ethiopia and from there to Europe, North America and Australia, beginning a large and widely dispersed Somali diaspora.

In 1992, drought resulted in a food shortage and mass starvation. When the rains returned, people suffered hepatitis, measles, dysentery, tuberculosis. Americans and Europeans, responding to the horrors they watched on evening television news programs, sent huge shipments of food and supplies to Somalia, but delivering the aid proved a dangerous undertaking. Ships stood offshore for weeks while armed bandits fought for control of materials to be unloaded. Thugs, all of them wielding machine guns, looted warehouses, hijacked relief conveys, emptied out supply centers for their own benefit. Even after desperately needy children and starving women did receive food, blankets, or anything of value, men descended upon them and forcefully took it away. To protect the men and women working in international aid agencies, the United Nations deployed several thousand peacekeepers to Somalia. The accelerating descent into anarchy was reaching a nadir and American military men, on a humanitarian mission, went in to restore order. They found themselves caught in the crossfire of interclan warfare, on television, and American sentiment turned against all efforts to alleviate the people's suffering. The Americans left, humiliated. The U.N. forces withdrew in 1995.

In 1994, I attended a conference in Paris of Somali expatriate political activists. I was the only non-Somali interested enough to stay beyond the formal opening speeches. As usual, the discussion degenerated into interclan squabbling. The few tolerant and rational men, the physicians and engineers and professors, were silenced. They withdrew from the discussion and returned to their new homes and careers.

What remains of Mrs. Miller's teaching, of the care and love she gave? Was her gift of knowledge forgotten, lost, blown away in the storm of Somalia's violence and dissolution? I think about Mrs. Miller's students, those bright young men who earnestly practiced and perfected their English in conversations with me. I wonder if they are alive. Perhaps with their skills and command of English they managed to survive. If alive and in Somalia, in normal times they would become community elders. Perhaps a few returned to their clan-family's land in the north, to a new and more limited Somaliland, and perhaps, because a talented and dedicated teacher focused on them when they were young they became better and wiser adults than they might otherwise have been. More likely, most are either dead or long ago joined the diaspora.

I wrote this in 2010, wishing I could look back at Mrs. Miller's projects and at the many ambitious development programs for Somalia during the 1960s and see some small measure of lasting benefit. I saw almost none. At least, Mrs. Miller was spared knowing of the chaos that destroyed the city she knew and loved so well.

MOGADISCIO: IN MEMORIAM

The stories in Tales of Mogadiscio were written in remembrance of a brief time in the life of the city. They tell of people who befriended me and made my life interesting and most agreeable. They express my love for the city itself, my wish that Mogadiscio be remembered for the delightful, charming place it once was and for what it might have become.

How do I describe the Mogadiscio I knew?

In 1960, Somalia gained its independence and Mogadiscio was designated by the United Nations as its capital. It was the largest by far and the best located city in the country, but in truth, other than for people in its immediate vicinity and tied into its economy, for most Somalis their future capital was a city in the distance they had heard about but never seen. The national government was even more distant as a concept and a concrete entity. It was a post-colonial institution constructed by foreign experts and a relatively small number of Somali men who had been specially educated by Europeans for their roles as senators and administrators. Most Somalis had little, if any, experience with the modern world they were expected to enter. The majority were pastoral nomads herding camels, sheep and goats across a vast semi-arid to arid landscape. A large minority of the population, about a third, were village farmers settled along and between two narrow rivers in southern Somalia. The small populations of urban Somalis, people of the few ancient coastal cities, remained separate and distinct from the pastoral nomads and the village farmers.

What sort of city did Somalis inherit as their capital city? I think of Mogadiscio before 1960 as a city composed of two urban communities living side-by-side, one modern and European, the other smaller, preserving traditions from centuries past. For most of the world Mogadiscio was the modern community, a twentieth century city created by Italians for Italian colonials. The smaller community, Hamar Wein,

15

was known only locally. It had been the original Mogadiscio, a thousand year old city famous for the cloth its people produced and as an important center of trade on the East Africa coast.

The Italian Mogadiscio was an outcome of Italian unification and Italy's nationalist drive to become a major European power, which in the 19th and early 20th centuries meant acquiring colonies. Ethiopia, conquered in the 1930s, was to be the Jewel in the Crown of the Second Roman Empire and Mogadiscio would be its port, connected to Addis Abba by a two-lane highway, La Strada Imperiale. Earlier, in the 1920s, an Italian Duke and entrepreneur had established a plantation in Mogadiscio's hinterland, a stable and productive company dependent upon the labor, often forced labor, and enterprise of Somalis. The development was considerable, including the damming of a river for irrigation, a railroad to Mogadiscio and an airstrip that later became Mogadiscio's airport.

By 1930 the cathedral had been built, Italians were living in Mogadiscio and Italian planners had designed an urban infrastructure for the colonial Mogadiscio intended for Italians only. Somali labor built the Italian Mogadiscio; Somalis were workers, artisans, soldiers and servants, but they did not live among the Italians nor did the Italians deal with them as equals.

The planners' vision was grand: a landscape of tree-lined streets laid out in a classic grid and set with heroic Italian buildings of stone. There was a Norman-Gothic Cathedral with twin towers; a Mediterranean compound where nuns and priests lived, kept a school for Italian children and an orphanage for abandoned offspring of Italian men and Somali women; the Governor's mansion across from the Cathedral; a triumphal arch through which the Italian king and his entourage entered the city in 1934, riding in stylish automobiles on the road from the new, deeper harbor; an imposing, fascist style red brick National Assembly; a post office; beautifully maintained parks and pavilions and public gardens; housing for Italian families and Italianate villas for the elite; schools for Italian children; an Italian bank; the Croce del Sud hotel; the Ospedale Martini hospital in a naturally sanitary location at the ocean shore; a fine Cinema Italia; luxurious recreation facilities; stores; restaurants; cafés. Along the central city streets were two and three storied arcaded, ornately detailed, perfectly proportioned buildings gleaming white against the blue sky.

As they built their city the Italians incorporated a number of the original Mogadiscio's historic buildings into their urban design, then they leveled what was in their way and of no particular interest to them. The Arba Rukun mosque, from 1269 C.E., became part of their city center. Preserved to serve as the new city's Museum was a 19th century Arabian residence with a three-story tower, two cannons at the entrance, a crenellated rooftop, a heavy wooden decorated door and an interior garden with a fountain at its center.

They left untouched the graceful curve of the original harbor. At the entrance to the city from the old harbor stood an octagonal shaped 19th century Zanzibar customs house built for officials to control merchants in their dhows as they came to trade in the original Mogadiscio. A few substantial older residences remained in the semicircle of land around the harbor, including a palace that continued as home for families whose founding ancestors had come from Oman. Other palaces were empty and slipping into ruin. In front of one lay a pile of stone cannon balls and, pointing toward the sea, two bronze cannons with a green patina, probably of Portuguese origin and similar to those in the 18th century Zanzibar fort. Below the palaces, at the shore, an open area of thorny vegetation and the remains of a low stone wall suggested a vanished stately garden.

Hamar Wein and a small nearby neighborhood, Shengani, is all that remains of the original Mogadiscio. Its people are obviously descended from a mixed ancestry, predominantly Somali but also Arab, Persian and other nations from afar.

17

According to tradition in Hamar Wein, one of its lineages, the Shanshia, is descended from men of Shiraz in Persia. Mogadiscio may mean Throne of the Shah. Somalis call Mogadiscio "Hamar" and everyone calls the indigenous Mogadiscio "Hamar Wein": Hamar meaning Red, possibly for a reddish skin color and Wein meaning Big.

Mogadiscio began in the 900s C.E. Its harbor, well suited for dhows and the early Portuguese ships, is located at the point where from November to March Indian Ocean monsoon winds come to the East Africa coast, flow down the coast to Sofala in Mozambique, then reverse from April to October and cut out again at Mogadiscio, back across the ocean. The city prospered for centuries as a productive economy, a market center for goods from the interior and, most importantly, as a destination for merchants from Egypt, the Middle East, the Arabian Peninsula, Persia, India, China, who sailed the monsoon and traded in the coastal city-states.

By the 1200s Mogadiscio's people had converted to Islam, giving them a written language, Arabic, a literature and contact with civilizations across the globe. In 1331, Ibn Battuta and his companions sailed into Mogadiscio's harbor and were received as guests. He wrote in detail about Mogadiscio as a city of vast resources, learned men, governing officials and a gracious lifestyle. In 1417, the Great Admiral of the Chinese Fleet, Zheng He, stopped in Mogadiscio and continued south to Malindi, Mombassa and Zanzibar. In 1497, Vasco de Gama, sailing from the south and on to India, recorded that Mogadiscio was a large city with four and five story houses, palaces in its centre and many mosques with cylindrical minarets.

When I walked along the streets of Hamar Wein, I often felt I could see into its past. There was, for example, the watching of a tel grow. Tel, Arabic for hill, is used in archeology as the term for a broad, flat hill with gently sloping sides, a shape that results from having been the site for many centuries of a city long since disappeared. Until modern building technologies a city inevitably rose above the ground on which it began. In the course of time, buildings collapsed or burned down and materials were left lying where they fell until, years later, another building rose or a road spread over the rubble that had long since fused with the soil. An archeologist can distinguish an abandoned residential site from a natural hill or mound. She will run a trench through the tel, expose the strata that grew through time and excavate, layer by layer.

I actually saw a tel in progress. I noticed under a number of houses in Hamar Wein a low space where goats and chickens were kept. One house had an under space only a foot or so high and people used it for trash disposal. As was explained to me, in the past the unpaved streets in front of houses gradually rose above the level of the doorstep. For each house, when the entrance door finally became uncomfortably low, the family vacated the ground floor and opened a door, with stairs, to the second floor. Eventually, another floor for the house would be built on the roof. For a time the ground floor was useful for keeping animals, but when the space became full with trash and silt and the street level had risen to the new first floor the family sealed off the original door. Thus, through the centuries the city rose imperceptibly, without changing form, above the land on which it began.

The central mosque for all Somalis, the Jama Mosque, stands at the edge of Hamar Wein. Its founding, as indicated by the date over the door, written in Arabic, was in the Islamic 616 Year of the Hijra, which corresponds to 1238 of the Common Era. A Somali friend introduced me to the Sheik. I stepped down with him from the street level on to a neatly swept paved area in front of the mosque entrance. The proportions of the arched entry and of the interior arches clearly indicated that the present floor lay well above the original floor of the structure. The Sheik said the mosque minaret was part of the original structure, with the stairs built of timber that was termite-proof and as strong as iron. We climbed the spiral staircase and looked out over the city.

In 1871, the Sultan of Zanzibar established control over Mogadiscio and its trade. In 1892, he leased the city to the Italians. In 1905, Italy purchased Mogadiscio from the Sultan.

With the Italian Mogadiscio fully built, Hamar Wein became, in effect, a walled-in casbah stretching from the road along the ocean, the Lungo Mare, inward to and behind tall, closely set buildings on Via Roma and Corso Vittorio Emanuele, the streets at its border with the Italian city. In Hamar Wein people continued their traditional ways amid the remnants of past glory. They lived in two- and three-story plastered and white-washed coral rock buildings along narrow streets, prayed in their own mosques and traded in their own markets. They dressed traditionally and many of their women were in the veil.

In 1949, Mogadiscio began a new phase of its history. For the following decade it functioned as the center where the United Nations, Italy, Britain, the United States and a large number of other countries based their programs for Somalia's socio-economic development. They brought in personnel and resources to prepare Somalis for independence. Italy's role in the process was key. At the end of World War II, the U.N. had stripped Italy of its colonies, then turned around and, in 1949, made it Trustee over its southern Somalia former colony. Concurrently, in northern Somalia, the former British colony became a British U.N. Protectorate with Hargeisa, a small town, as its administrative center. Based in Mogadiscio, the Trusteeship Administration proceeded to develop Somali governmental institutions, educational facilities and economic infrastructure. Somalis participating in the development process focused immediately and primarily on issues concerning politics and government. Clan-based political parties grew in number and engaged actively, often contentiously, with the U.N. Advisory Council in the larger public debate.

On July 1, 1960, Italian Somaliland and British Somaliland joined to form the Somali Republic.

By the early 1960s the government was functioning and development aid was flowing. This was the Mogadiscio I knew. It was the capital of a new country, full of promise. Embassies, twenty-six in a city of some 100,000 people, were already well established, modern hotels had been built and businesses prospered. For the continually arriving foreign experts and their families, houses enclosed in compound walls ringed the downtown and ranged along the oceanfront. Somali businessmen and government officials moved into Italian houses or, as they accumulated wealth, built their own modern style homes. Pastoral nomads were coming in from the bush to settle into wattle-daub houses in and around the well-established Somali neighborhoods at Mogadiscio's borders. On the west and north of the city were Elgab, Bondere and Hodon. Villagio Arabo was to the east, a *quartier* of Somali and Yemeni families and a small community from the Haudramaut region of southern Arabia.

Mogadiscio was growing. Despite political agitation behind the scene, living was comfortable. The city was vibrant and hopeful.

In 1969, Mogadiscio again changed in form and dynamic. The army, well equipped by the Soviet Union, took over the government; "scientific socialism" and Russian influence dominated. Non-communist countries, except for Italy, minimized their presence in Somalia, while the Soviet Union supported literacy programs, enrollment in schools, health care services and experiments in rural development. Mogadiscio grew with new public buildings and grand monuments. Somalis from all regions of the country arrived, transforming the city. Small businesses thrived. Money flowed into Mogadiscio and remittances from men working in Arab countries brought in cash and goods. From the interriverine farms came food and charcoal for cooking and an abundant supply of qat, an herb with an amphetamine effect.

By the late 1970s, Mogadiscio was still growing, mostly in population. It sprawled, swollen and overwhelmed by a flood of Somalis fleeing warfare, seeking refuge and becoming refugees. By 1980, again responding to Cold War politics, the Somali government had changed its alliance from the Soviet Union to the United States. Drought, governmental corruption and clan warfare were devastating the people and Mogadiscio's educated middle class was beginning a flight into exile. By the late '80s the country was moving toward all-encompassing warfare between clans and sub-clans.

In 1991, the government fell as its dictator fled and Somalia's descent into anarchy began. Well-armed Somali clansmen who had together defeated the dictator became rivals and fought one another on the streets of Mogadiscio. Pastoral nomadic warriors from central Somalia, men with no experience of city life set to destroying an urban terrain alien to them. They machined-gunned and blew up fine buildings and infrastructure. Many of the clansmen moved into Hamar Wein, taking anything they wanted, including women. Throughout Mogadiscio people were caught in the crossfire, to be killed or maimed. Many were forced to flee the city and seek a life elsewhere as refugees. Somali men and boys turned the city into a war ravaged landscape.

Mogadiscio's colonial architecture remains as pockmarked shells of buildings or has vanished. Its ancient mosques and Arabian buildings stand neglected, untended, falling apart. In this time of overwhelming misery these are the least of anyone's worries, but, perhaps, in the future, in a time when peace has returned, Somalis will learn of the damage done to their heritage and realize what treasure has been lost.

OUR FAMILY IN MOGADISCIO

In the early years of our marriage my husband, Raj, informed me on more than one occasion that I had no understanding of family. He assured me he had no complaint about me as a wife and mother; he said he was speaking analytically, not pejoratively. At the time I hardly knew what he meant, other than the obvious fact that he and I viewed family from different perspectives. He had grown up in India as the first born and first son in a large, close, bourgeois, well-educated family. Excepting our children and me, the meaningful people throughout his life remained his parents, his sister and, especially, his brothers and sister. He stayed in contact with uncles, aunts and cousins. Neither he nor his brothers showed any interest whatsoever in having a close, long-term friendship outside the family. I had grown up without a mother and with a father who provided me with the basics of life but little else. I was a White American Great Depression baby from the lower working class. During most of my childhood I lived with strangers. I had no siblings, no aunts or uncles or cousins. My grandfather treated me kindly. His second wife loved me and I called her Grandmother. In place of kin I had friends and teachers and churchwomen who cared about me. When Raj's brothers came to live with us so they could attend university, Raj and I both welcomed them but differently. He was acting within his role as eldest brother; I thought of his brothers as potential friends.

I had yet to learn the significant differences between family, friendship and in-laws.

It was during the first year we lived in Mogadiscio that family and friendship began to take on a new dimension for Raj and me. He had finished his Ph.D. and was teaching in a Midwestern university when, in 1963, he received a substantial post-doctoral research grant to study the politics and government of Somalia. He, our seven-year-old son, five-year-old daughter and I moved to Mogadiscio and within months of our settling in I had complicated our family life. I befriended a child and brought him into our home. The boy had a family. Not only a family. He had a community and they became part of our lives, as well.

Our travel to Mogadiscio was a great adventure. Raj planned the trip for us, first to London, where we stayed with the first brother who had lived with us, on across Europe and then to India. At long last Raj was presenting his wife and children to family, and I saw the places that had been home to him before his graduate school days in America. We stayed two weeks with his mother, father and sweet, vivacious sister, plus a bewildering abundance of aunts, uncles, cousins, nieces, nephews, aunts and uncles by marriage, second cousins, second cousins once removed.

One evening about midway through our visit, at a party for kin and kindred, the sister took me aside. She looked beautiful in her blue silk, gold-bordered sari, but when I began complimenting her, she stopped me. "I have something serious to say. Last night only you asked about the family arrangements for my marriage. Do you remember I said nothing? Because what I truly want is to live with you the way my brothers did. Would you accept that?

"I would love having you with us. And so would the children. You are so good with them and they absolutely adore you."

"Would it be possible for me to enroll in your university?"

"Of course! You should go on to graduate school. Your brothers did. Why not you?"

"I will help you with cooking and the children. I mean it, truly. But first we will need Papaji's permission. Will my going to America cost too much money?"

"We can work it out. What about all that jewelry for your dowry? I'm amazed at how much you pay here for gold; twice as much as in the States, maybe more. You might as well sell the pure gold stuff right away and use the money for plane fare. Besides, Indian jewelry doesn't go with American clothes so you won't wear it anyhow, once you get there. You'll be mostly in blue jeans and knitted tops. You'll see."

She uttered a distressed "Oh!" Her hands slipped up and over her ornate gold necklace and earrings and she nervously readjusted the shoulder folds of her sari.

I spoke no more of jewelry. "Don't worry. Raj and I will talk with Papaji and Mamaji for you. We'll persuade them to send you to Mogadiscio next August, just before we're ready to leave. We can all go together to America. We'll be a family of five going home."

As our visit in India was coming to an end, Raj and I decided that he should go first, alone, to Somalia. We knew no one there and had very little information about Mogadiscio. It would have been unwise for us to arrive with two small children, too much luggage and no idea of where we would live. We thought it best that he explore the city and locate suitable accommodations for us while I looked after the children in the safe haven of his parent's home.

He left for Mogadiscio by airplane, promising to send a telegram when all was ready.

In Mogadiscio, to his great surprise, Raj encountered Indian men on the streets and in the stores. They greeted him warmly, recognizing him as one of their own. He looked like them and, like them, spoke Hindustani and English. Although they were Muslim and knew from his name that he was of Hindu origin, they never asked his religion or caste. They accepted him unconditionally. They found a house in a good compound for him to rent. They showed him where to shop, where to bank, what services were available. They forgave him for buying a battered Fiat 600 at a ridiculously high price and from an Italian. Raj had not even bargained! The

Indians felt humiliated. An Indian, a man like themselves, had been outwitted by an Italian.

We have a picture postcard of Mogadiscio Raj sent to our son and daughter in Bombay. He wrote, "... Yesterday I went out of the city and saw wild baboons and camels. You can also see wild giraffe and elephants if you go 100 miles to the south. Today I saw a United Arab Airlines Comet jet fly over the city. Everybody here speaks Somali and Italian. Very few speak English, and you will have to learn to speak Somali or Italian. There is a very nice beach on the Indian Ocean and we will go swimming. There are no sharks near the beach but far away..." The ink has faded and we can no longer read the end of the sentence.

After a few weeks, Raj arranged for the children and me to fly Air India from Bombay, over the sea and a golden Arabian desert. We landed on a Thursday evening in Aden, Yemen, still a major British port for its colonial empire. The children and I slept well in our hotel and the next morning ate a hearty English breakfast. My memory of Aden is slight, except for having wandered in the hot sun, searching for a post office, lost on wide, empty streets, then my sudden realization that we were in a Muslim land and this was the Friday Sabbath. The post office would be closed. At last we saw one person, an adolescent boy dressed in the traditional white ankle length shirt with long sleeves, the dishdasha, holding a large goat by its ear. I approached the boy and asked for directions. He did not speak but gestured for us to follow. He stayed well ahead of the children and me with his goat, glancing back to see if we were still with him, leading us to the edge of the British *quartier*. At this spot he stopped and with a slight farewell bow turned and walked back toward his own *quartier*.

On Saturday morning we boarded an Aden Airways turbo-prop jet headed to Mogadiscio and our home for nearly a year.

I liked Mogadiscio immediately. It was a delightful city, lovingly constructed and carefully maintained, still intact after the demise of colonialism and a good place to live, especially if one had a decent income in a hard currency and reliable ties to the outside world. It was prospering as the capital of the newly independent Somalia, bustling and brimming with embassies and development projects, with the bright accoutrements of modernity, plus a multinational, multilingual array of foreigners who had come to manage, direct and dispense.

We settled into our small house and within a few days our first visitors, four of Raj's friends from the Indian community, came calling. I watched from inside the doorway as he met them at our compound gate, guided them to the circle of chairs under the bougainvillea arbor and answered earnest questions I could not quite hear. Then he gestured for me to come and meet the gentlemen.

I appeared and the men froze. They stared at me, wordlessly.

"Raj, you didn't tell them your wife is American?"

"Sorry, I forgot."

I was about to shake hands with our guests but caught myself and used the Indian namaste gesture instead, hands together, raised to the face, head inclined forward.

The oldest man said "Salaam Alei'kum"

I responded, "Alei'kum Salaam. Please sit and I will bring tea."

To me, the men looked North Indian, but with a cautious, watchful way about them I had not seen often in India. They wore the conventional urban outfit of men everywhere: trousers, white shirt, shoes. The two older men sported a neatly trimmed beard, signifying membership in their Muslim Shia community. They conversed in fluent English with an occasional Hindi or Arabic word thrown in to spice its meaning.

27

They had brought a boy along with them, a nice looking child, slender and well built, dressed neatly in a white shirt, short beige trousers, rubber sandals. I thought him to be a few years older than my son, about ten years old. His large expressive dark eyes held my attention. He stood quietly behind the man I assumed was his father and when the conversation began he went to the driveway, found a smooth, hard-packed place in the soil, brought a handmade top from his pocket and set it to spinning as he watched and listened.

The next day the men and the boy, plus an elderly gentleman, arrived in time for afternoon tea. Raj welcomed them in and they sat down purposefully.

The elderly man spoke for the group. He addressed Raj. "We understand your wife is a teacher. We would like her to teach in our Indian school."

Raj said, "Why don't you ask her?" and they all looked at me.

I hesitated. "Does that mean you want me to teach your children? I've never taught anyone younger than 18 years old."

"You are a teacher. Why can you not teach our boys?"

"I suppose I can, but I need some time to think about it."

As the men were leaving, the boy with the beautiful eyes came to me, courteous and very serious. I leaned over and he whispered in my ear, "My name is Azad. Will you be my teacher?"

I said, in a low voice, just to him, "I'd like very much to be your teacher."

Nevertheless, I did need time. First on my list of things to do was enrolling our son and daughter into the American Embassy primary school. It was an excellent school with good teachers. The children did well in their lessons and were happy with new friends. They also made friends with children of the

United Nations families who lived near us. Raj was soon busy with work he obviously enjoyed and our house and daily routine became orderly and at least somewhat predictable.

After meeting more of the Indian men and their wives, I decided to accept the offer to teach their boys. I had come to Mogadiscio eager to know the city and the position of teacher in a local school would give me respectability, a role, a legitimate reason to talk and visit with people. Besides, I had half promised Azad.

Best of all, the Indian community lived in the most interesting part of Mogadiscio, its casbah, the original Mogadiscio. The Somalis call it Hamar Wein. The Indian homes, their mosque and most of the shops they owned were in Hamar Wein, a crowded, exotic *quartier*, a seemingly impenetrable agglomeration of two- and three-story white buildings and market places set along streets that were barely more than a pathway wide. It was not a place most foreigners or Italian colonials knew or would want to know. The school in which I was to teach Azad was in Hamar Wein, attached to the mosque.

Azad was a creature of Hamar Wein. From early childhood he had roamed its streets, running and playing with other Indian boys. He had been schooled for a few years, attending the Indian madressa with boys his age, learning religion and religious rituals, arithmetic, reading and writing in several languages for religious texts and for business, being prepared for his future as a shopkeeper and a devout member of the Indian community.

In the madressa and later, in the shop, boys in the community learned bookkeeping, how to write business letters in two languages, keep bank accounts in Mogadiscio and abroad, fill out a voucher. When goods arrived by ship from Aden, Italy, India, China, they would know how to read and sign the bill of lading, how to keep records of the merchandise in a shop. The boys became literate in the manner of a merchant community; they read business related materials and the Koran and booklets about their religion. Reading for pleasure or general knowledge was not a highly held value. Even if such books and magazines had been available, the boy would have no place to sit and read them. He most likely would not go to a library; the only library in Mogadiscio, the one provided by the United States Information Service (USIS), was on a street in the Italian part of town, socially a significant distance from Hamar Wein. He could not sit at home during the day doing "nothing" as casually reading a book would be perceived, because the house during the day was meant for women and girls. A boy belonged outside, doing the things expected of men and boys; he would not want to be known as a house-hen.

An Indian boy in Hamar Wein filled his time with other Indian boys until his twelfth or thirteenth year. At that age he joined the men, usually working behind the counter of his father's or an uncle's shop in or near Hamar Wein. By the time he was eighteen his marriage, always to a girl from the same community, would have been arranged for him. When his first child, preferably a son, was born he became a man, a full adult expected to play throughout his lifetime the family and kinship roles he had inherited by being born into the community. Any flair for individuality was ordinarily repressed. If nonconformity surfaced within their midst, friends, even family, shunned and gossiped about the offending person until repentance was demonstrated. Struggling against the general will only ensnared a person ever more tightly in its web. In this world of poverty few opportunities existed for exit to safety elsewhere.

Azad was different from the other boys I knew and observed in his community. He was not designed for working in a shop. There had been talk of sending him to Q'um in Iran to study religion but he showed no enthusiasm for the religious life. Perhaps he felt adrift, bored, no longer one of the little boys, not yet on his way to adulthood. He had always been something of a loner, with an unusual streak of independence. He was the son of a woman who was an outsider; she had been brought from Pakistan as a bride at the age of 14. Only he, with a few other boys, ventured outside Hamar Wein, playing hide and seek in the arcades of buildings along Corso Vittorio Emanuele, running on the sandy Lido beach and splashing in the water, sufficiently independent that his father allowed him to shop for the family in the Elgab market and to find his way alone across the city to my compound gate. A few men warned me, "You watch. Azad could turn bad." I rather doubted that but could imagine him not conforming totally to their idea of how a really good boy would behave.

Having decided to teach the boys, especially Azad, my next step was to discover the route I would take from our house, through the city, to the classroom. Each day, after Ahmed, our guard, had opened our compound gate for the day; after Asha, the woman who helped me keep house, had returned from market and we had the kitchen in order, after Raj had driven our children to their school in his sputtering little Fiat 600 and was occupied with his research I set forth. I walked from our compound high on a bluff behind the city, on to a dusty road, down a narrow paved street lined with residences set behind high walls topped with broken glass, past the National Assembly, into the Italian core of Mogadiscio.

The city streets, two lanes wide, were paved, and trees shaded the sidewalks. Pedestrian traffic was heavy and automobile traffic fairly light. Most of the cars on the roads were three-wheeled auto rickshaws and Fiat 1100 taxis; only the foreigners and a few elite Somalis owned their own personal automobiles. Goods were hauled in small Fiat trucks or on a flat, two-wheeled donkey cart, too often with its driver mercilessly wielding a long pole to poke the poor beast and set it braying.

While walking along the main streets I overheard bits of conversation in a rich variety of languages. Somalis, Italians, local Indian and Arab men, families of all nationalities from the many embassies and U.N. agencies strolled from one Italian establishment to another. They lingered under the trees to greet one another and chat. In the cafés and wherever one could sit comfortably, young Somali men, quite presentable, sat and talked, rather loudly, as people in the open countryside often do, totally relaxed. I imagined them in their homeland sitting in the shade of an acacia tree, talking and arguing as they were doing in the Mogadiscio cafés.

Surprisingly, considering the large number of men walking about, Mogadiscio streets did not smell of urine, as did congested streets in so many of the cities I visited during those years. Apparently, we in Mogadiscio benefited from mosques having a urinal and water for the men to use.

Given Somalia's poverty relatively few beggars waylaid the affluent. When a foreigner parked his car on the main street, "watch boys," all of them abandoned children, descended on him, saying "I watch, I watch," and he gave them protection money in the form of small change. I knew little about the boys. The Indians told me they lived together and took care of one another. At night they slept inside building arcades, mostly on the street behind the Cathedral. A few Somali men with shrunken limbs, labeled "spider men" by foreigners, crawled from place to place, stopping to ask for alms. They were victims of polio or had been born clubfoot. An occasional emaciated woman held out a cupped hand, pleading for a coin.

My destination was an area beyond the city center and the Italian stores. I walked along Via Roma, past a hotel, past a cinema, past the Indian and Arab shops and turned left onto a pathway between two buildings, leaving behind the Italian Mogadiscio. Thus I reached Hamar Wein.

Azad's community, about a thousand persons, was, when I knew them, three generations in Hamar Wein and Merca, a small coastal city south of Mogadiscio. Most of the men were shopkeepers. In their one room stores they sold all manner of household and personal goods: shoes, sandals, tableware, cooking implements, cloth, clothing, hammers, nails, clocks and on and on. Shelves lined the walls to the ceiling and were solidly packed with boxes of things to sell. More merchandise was kept in the go-down, a storage place below the shop floor. The owner and his assistant, preferably a son, sat behind the counter. When I asked twelve-year old Indian boys what they wanted to be when they grew up, they answered, "I want to sit in my shop and work very hard."

Like nearly all the Indian families, Azad's family lived in an apartment in a three story building in Hamar Wein. I walked there from behind their building and sometimes paused to watch the Somali weavers working their looms in the shade of a large rush covered canopy fastened at two corners to the wall and two corners on poles. Each of the ten or so gaunt, probably tubercular men sat in a shallow pit, his loom stretched out in front of him, several inches above the ground. I once saw a small spinning wheel on the ground and asked to buy it but the weaver was unwilling to sell. I heard that women spun cotton at home and men dyed the fabric. Even with imported fabrics dominating the market they were still producing the cotton cloth Mogadiscio had traded for centuries throughout the Indian Ocean region and as far away as Egypt.

Unlike many Hamar Wein families, Azad's had electric lighting and piped-in water, plus the added advantage of an ocean front view. As in all the community's families, the mother and girls kept strict purdah; they were allowed to leave the apartment only when wearing the burqa, a loose dark garment that covered a woman from head to toe. As she walked outside she viewed the world through a peephole cut and crocheted into the burqa's face cover.

The community centered on their shops, their mosque and ties between the extended families. The women visited with kinswomen. The men spent much of their time in the mosque. Each morning, they rose with the sun, dressed and walked to their mosque to pray. Many stayed on to drink tea and talk with other men from the community. Religious ceremonies were frequent and elaborate. Governing took place through men meeting, making decisions under the leadership of the older men and forming committees to address community issues and concerns.

The world-view of Azad's community was narrow, but the number of languages mastered by nearly all the men was phenomenal. Azad knew a little English when I met him. He spoke his mother tongue within the community, a second Indian language with Indians not from his community, a third Indian language for business correspondence and record keeping, Somali for the streets and with Somalis, Italian because it was the colonial language. In the mosque he learned Arabic for the Koran and Urdu for the Shia religious books.

The community's school in which I taught was a secular school, but different from any I had known. Physically, it consisted of one room in a building adjoining the Indian mosque, furnished with roughly made wooden student desks and a rickety cabinet. The books for the students were inadequate and out-of-date.

As a teacher I was replacing two Muslim Indians, a married couple hired from Nairobi, both trained teachers and graduates of Makerere University in Kampala. Muslim Indians in Nairobi, and in most of the cities of British East Africa, were far more progressive than the Mogadiscio Indians. Very few kept purdah. The woman teacher refused to wear a burqa and the Mogadiscio men complained. The couple also refused to live in Hamar Wein. When a thief broke into their house and stole the woman's gold jewelry, adding financial loss to insult, she decided she could not stay. The couple packed up and went to London. The school committee replaced them with two Somali teachers, both men, Sharif and Adan. Adan belonged to a pastoral nomad lineage and, like most Somalis, had neither interest in nor sympathy for the culture of cities. Sharif came from Brava, another of the ancient coastal towns, and was himself a member of an urban community.

Each morning, to reach the mosque and the school, I walked through Hamar Wein's maze of streets and paths. They were unpaved and narrow. The flat-roofed residences, shops and small mosques were constructed of coral rock, then plastered and whitewashed. Nearly all the finely carved doors and lintels that once decorated the houses had long since disappeared, probably bought as antiques by the first Italians in the city. For all the dilapidated state of nearly everything, the jumble of stone walls and white forms still pleased the eye. I could imagine the old city paved, cleaned and restored.

The Indian mosque and school were in the center of Hamar Wein. After a few days I could find my way there without getting lost. About twenty boys were waiting for me in the classroom. I had assumed, from their size and frame that they were nine or ten years old but when Ramadan began they all fasted. Children usually do not fast so I asked their ages, to discover that all were twelve or older. This being my first experience with living outside the United States I was used to the look of children who were raised on a high protein diet and with modern medical care. I had even underestimated Azad's age. I was surprised to discover that he also was twelve years old. During the following years, living with us, he took on the height and build of a typical American teenager.

Sharif, Adan and I decided I would teach science. Discipline was my first problem. The boys reacted differently from any students I had ever known. In the classroom, when I stood facing them they eagerly tried to please me, sitting obediently still, raising their hands to ask questions. When I turned my attention even slightly away from them, they threw pencils, shoved and nettled one another with rude sounding words, snickered and tittered. How could I teach these boys? I watched my fellow teachers and visited two madressas where teachers of Arabic held their pupils' attention and led them into learning. I could not change my style completely, to rap knuckles or use a quick flick of a switch on an upturned palm, but I stopped smiling at the boys and regularly leveled a cool, hard tone of voice at them.

Other, more basic, problems soon became evident. The boys were not ready for a modern school, but never having taught children, I could not judge their grade level and did not know what subject matter a proper primary school teacher would have presented to them. They all spoke some English but not well enough for it to be the medium of instruction. Additionally, I had no textbook from which to teach.

I talked with the community's school committee about the poor quality of the teaching materials and soon learned that the men were sharply divided about how the school should be run. In fact, the committee was divided on whether a secular school was at all necessary. The older men believed that their madressa, with its instruction in religion and Arabic and Urdu, plus bookkeeping skills, had been good enough for them and was all the next generation would ever need. A secular school was the idea of the committee's younger men. The older men went along, but reluctantly, and were unwilling to invest in equipment or proper textbooks from Nairobi, the nearest world-connected urban center.

I proceeded to teach as best I could. Azad was my one true student. With the other boys I was never certain what was happening. I presented facts and explained ideas without knowing how they were perceived. I discovered, for example, that the boys had no concept of a microscopic world and, of course, I had no microscope to show them what they cannot otherwise see, only drawings of one-celled plants and animals that for them could not have been convincing pictures of reality. Nevertheless, I continued teaching the basics of biology, using available books and my imagination. One day I took our family's large magnifying glass to class with me, along with a sponge, as part of a lesson on differences between plants and animals. The boys passed the sponge around, examining it through the magnifying glass, continuing, I thought, the lesson in their own language.

One boy paused and asked me, "How many shillings you pay for the sponge?"

I told him. He returned to the animated discussion with the group. Then he said to me, "You pay too much. Next time, you ask me. You buy wholesale from the shop of my father." So much for the science lesson.

Azad was a delight. He responded to information and ideas, asked questions, understood explanations. I could focus on him in deciding what and how to teach all the boys. I depended upon the small but marvelous U.S.I.S. library, the only library, perhaps, in all of Somalia after the British Council library was shut down and its books torn apart so the pages could be used as wrapping paper in stalls where food and dry goods were sold. I checked out children's books and learned, or relearned, about the sciences and how to devise simple experiments. If my experiment of the day, such a demonstration of why an airplane flies, worked out especially well, the boys applauded; they had been well entertained. Most of all, they loved for me to read Dr. Seuss books to them. "Green Eggs and Ham" was their favorite.

I had been teaching in the school for about two months when, one morning, I arrived to total disorder. The boys were running in circles, manic, shouting incoherently. They had upended the desks, jumped on them, cracked the tops and broken the legs. While the others cheered him on, the wildest boy was tearing pages out of their ragged old books and tossing them in the air.

Only Azad was still. He sat on the doorstep, head in hands, fighting back tears. I asked, "What is wrong?" and he replied, "Now I will never go to school."

The school committee had closed the school. The older men had decided that their sons and grandsons knew all they needed to know to buy and sell and keep books, to marry and raise a family according to tradition as understood by the older men. No amount of persuasion from the younger men could change their minds.

I stood looking at this sad, lost child who was being denied a most basic need in life. And to me, school was a basic need. It had been central to my very existence. Teachers and librarians had paid attention to me and they approved of me. I could not imagine life without being either a student or a teacher.

I had to do something for Azad. I told him to come to my house and we would figure out what that something might be. The next day he was at the gate of our compound. Raj went and asked the boy why he was standing there. "I want to see my teacher." Raj welcomed him in. I introduced him to the children and he stayed with them for about an hour, talking, quietly observing us.

When he was ready to leave I went with him to the gate and watched him as he walked away. He had pushed his white Muslim cap forward at a rakish angle over his forehead and his step was jaunty, as if he were singing a lively tune to himself.

Azad soon became a member of our household. I felt that his mother, Zeynab, should know me and be reassured about our family. I visited her and the sisters in their family apartment in Hamar Wein, and she and the girls visited me. Often, after the father left home in the morning for the mosque and his shop, Azad called a taxi, huddled his mother and sisters into it, and brought them to my house. Zeynab and the oldest girl came in burqa. The little girls wore dresses. A call of "purdah ladies" went up from the gate and the men disappeared. My guests rushed from the taxi, across the compound, through the door of the house. Once inside Zeynab threw back the face cover of her burqa and peered out between the slats of the louvered wall to see the place under the bougainvillea arbor where her husband and sons sat when they visited Raj. I served tea and biscuits and Azad translated for us.

Azad's father, older brother and other men from the Indian community came regularly to visit with Raj and me. They would stop by our house in the late afternoon, when the air was cool enough for taking a stroll, and have tea with us. They advised us on where to shop for what and how much to pay. We talked about India and Pakistan and compared customs of the British, Americans and Italians. A particularly interesting topic of conversation, especially for one of the younger men, Hussein, was explaining their religious practices and beliefs for my benefit. I listened with great interest. They knew to avoid talking with me about women's roles and rights.

In one of his discourses Hussein talked at length about Jews. He mentioned no Jew by name nor any specific action taken by Jews; he spoke in the abstract about treachery, greed, lying and such evil. He said they knew from the Koran that Jews wanted to kill the Prophet Mohammed. He told me that everyone in his community disapproved, in principle, of all Jews. Since their holy book shares much of its history with the Bible, I had already heard something of this nonsense. My annoyance was obvious. I reminded Hussein that Muslims also say good things about Jews because they are People of the Book. I said, "Think about it. The Koran and the Bible are from another time; their message must be interpreted for our time. Jews are people, some good, some bad, but just people. Simply another community."

For two weeks no Indian men came to our house. Then one day they reappeared.

We welcomed them in, asked them to be seated. I was returning from the kitchen when I overheard Hussein say to

Raj, "Please, excuse me, but ... Well, you see, my father and uncle told me to ask you something about the Signora ..."

I stepped forward and stared at him.

He was flustered. "We only want to know. Is she Jewish?"

An older man spoke. "Please understand. We are devout Muslims. If you are Jewish, we cannot step into your house. If we take food from your hand, we must pray and wash seven times to become clean again."

I thought this peculiar. I had never heard such a thing from my Turkish or Palestinian or Indonesian Muslim friends and suspected they would not have recognized the belief.

Raj shook his head, as if in disbelief. "Don't worry. She isn't Jewish."

I felt justified in mocking them a little. "Please accept these glasses of tea and these biscuits from the hands of a non-Muslim. I'm glad you're back. Let's talk about something else. ... But wait." I asked Azad, "What do you think about Jews?"

He reflected for a minute and answered, "There are two Jewish families in Mogadiscio. They do not make trouble. They do not cheat. They are okay."

Raj looked at me in surprise. He said, "That is a sensible boy."

Increasingly, Azad became a friend and companion on my daily rounds of the city, after we had solved a problem. He insisted upon walking two steps behind me because in his community a man or older boy walks behind his women to protect them. I told him I was an adult and did not need pro-tection. Next, he had to show respect. I said his walking behind me made conversation awkward, and I felt silly going about with a child in tow. I told him he was no longer a little boy who must demonstrate subordination to adults. Since his everyday language lacked a vocabulary for stages of youth between childhood and adulthood, I explained, "You are a big boy now. Not a big, big boy, but a big boy" and the phrase became our private joke. He accepted walking beside me and began in earnest as my interpreter. Only once did I correct him. He was repeating for my benefit what Somali men said about me as we walked by them on the street. I informed him, emphatically, that I did not want to know. I could not stop the lewd remarks, so I might as well not hear them.

From the beginning of Azad coming into our home, I had insisted that he finish the workbooks he had begun in the classroom. In the meantime, I was trying to find another school for him. I went first to the Italian school in Mogadiscio. They would not accept him because at twelve years old he was over the age of admission. Next, I approached the Americans but the American school at that time accepted only American children and a few children of top-level Somali government officials. Those were the only local schools available.

Therefore, plan three. I would teach Azad at home and bring him up to his grade level. Then I would convince his community that they should send him to Nairobi to live with a family from their Shia community and attend an English medium school there.

I set up a classroom, a table and chairs, under the bougainvillea arbor. Other than Friday, when Azad had mosque, and on days when the children were home from school, as soon as I had set the house in order he and I began class. Azad studied for half an hour, had a badminton break, which we played on the driveway for ten minutes, and he returned to work. He would spend four hours in our little school. I borrowed textbooks from the children's teachers, began with the second grade books and marched him through each grade to the end of the sixth. He learned quickly. As his English improved, he

41

played with the words and punned to amuse us. I learned as I taught him. It was fun.

Within six months Azad was ready, and I asked Raj to present my Nairobi school plan to Azad's father. The father was surprised but pleased with the idea; he said he had to discuss it with the elders in the mosque. He had no family in Nairobi and would need assistance. The elders took only one day to decide against school for Azad. They disapproved of any education beyond what was available in Mogadiscio. Azad's older brother had been hurt by the bias. Years before, the father had taken him to family in Pakistan for schooling, but when the boy returned to Mogadiscio for Ramadan vacation the father yielded to the opinion of others and kept him home, forever embittered by the deprivation.

Azad became despondent and I felt frustrated in the extreme. My prize student would end up nowhere, without an education, with horizons too limited for his talents and personality.

As Raj and I puzzled over what to do next, we received a letter from Bombay. Raj's father informed Raj that his sister had decided against going to the States. Instead, she would be married. Her aunts and cousins had convinced her that she would be happier as a wife and mother in India than as a graduate student in a foreign land.

A space in our home was empty. Raj's brothers had moved on and the sister would not be replacing them. And so it happened that, one day, as I was trying to imagine what else I could do to arrange schooling for Azad, Raj turned to me and said, "Do you want to take him home with us?" I immediately said, "Yes."

For Raj, bringing a boy into our household was a perfectly natural thing to do. In his extended family any fairly prosperous branch of the family in a large city, one with quality schools and opportunities for employment, would take care of a country cousin or nephew or, in later times, a niece, who stayed with them for a good long time until he finished his schooling or found a job. Although gratitude should be expressed, no one expected that a special bond would necessarily have been forged between the persons involved. Extended families operated that way; among kin help was given and received. Friendships may, or may not, have formed but remained irrelevant as to whether assistance was offered or accepted. On occasions when I thanked my in-laws in India for their kind hospitality they responded, "Fulfilling my obligations brings me happiness." The fact that Azad was not from family stretched the model, but that was all right with Raj. Our family knew his family well, they were Indian and they accepted me.

Our son and daughter liked Azad. They probably viewed him as another one of their father's family who came to spend time with us but better because he played with them.

My own mindset about Azad as part of our family was simple. As a child without a mother and an often-absent father I had lived with different families. Why shouldn't Azad do the same? I knew of no reason why Azad would not flourish in our tender care. School was terribly important to him, as it had been to me. We could provide him with both schooling and a home.

Back home, several close friends criticized me for removing a child from his natural home, and they had a valid point. I had to remind myself that without an education Azad would not have done well in life, especially in Somalia. By temperament he was not like the other boys. They defined themselves as merchants and took great pleasure in buying and selling. Even as children they sharpened their skills. Regularly, as one of their recreational activities, a few of the more adventurous older boys went in the morning to an Italian gift shop and bought an expensive box of Belgian chocolates. From there they walked to the Italian secondary school and, over the lunch hour, when the Italian students were playing outside, sold the chocolates one by one. The profit made was a measure of their accomplishment. Azad told me he never succeeded in such business transactions. He had once bought a broken bicycle that he repaired and sold. He lost money in the gambit and for months the boys teased him about his incompetence.

The morning after Raj and I decided we would offer to take him with us to America and send him to school, we explained to Azad what we had in mind. He said that would be fine with him. He agreed to the proposal. And why not? He liked us. He wanted to go to school. As I reflect on those days, I doubt that he fully grasped the fact that going to America entailed leaving his family and Mogadiscio.

That afternoon, when the father and brother came to the house for tea, we told them. At first there was not much to discuss. The idea shocked everyone, including us. We were far from being wealthy. In fact, we lived on Raj's modest professor's salary and my part-time teaching as a lecturer. Unlike many faculty couples, we did not have affluent parents to subsidize our dignified but low-income academic lifestyle. We were simply young and optimistic and naïve about the difficulties, as well as the benefits, for Azad and for us of taking him, at his age, into a world totally different from his own and, though we did not know it then, into the expatriate lifestyle we would soon adopt.

If Zeynab and the girls had not welcomed our proposal, I would not have known what to do. Zeynab said to me, "You will take good care of my son."

As Azad's family and the Indian community absorbed the implications of our proposal, a storm of gossip and specula-tion raged through the community. Only a few men thought Azad fortunate to have this opportunity. A man who had grown up in Zaila, a town on the Red Sea, had attended school in Nairobi for eight years and he valued education. Azad's older brother said he approved. However, many of the men protested; they said that Azad would "lose his reli-gion" meaning, in essence, he would eventually break his ties with them and the community. Several younger men spread rumors that we were taking Azad to be our servant or we wanted him as a husband for our daughter, who was at that time five years old. Two men took me aside to inform me that Azad was a bad boy, a troublemaker. Each suggested I take one of his sons instead.

How Azad's father decided he would allow Azad to leave with us and live in a far away country I do not know. His manner was inward. It was not his style to lead a conversation and he seldom added his words to what others were saying. I know he had consulted with family and friends. After some time he gave his consent and we began preparations.

The first matter to be settled was a passport for Azad. We had not anticipated the difficulties we would encounter. The Somali government had granted citizenship, with the accompanying right to a Somali passport, to only one Indian man. The others traveled on Indian or Pakistani passports.

What does citizenship mean in a tribal society? Except for the small merchant communities in the few urban centers, Somalia was society of clans. They had a system of unwritten laws enforced by tradition and an informal council of elders, but until an independent Republic of Somalia was instituted in 1960, they had never been governed within an overarching political, governmental structure. The idea of a formal government was new for them. Somalis depended upon the United Nations experts stationed in Mogadiscio to establish their government and train Somalis to become government officials. In the meantime, their thinking and worldview remained tribal.

If Azad were not a tribal Somali, what, then, was his nationality and what was to be his citizenship? Culturally he was Indian, but because his community had converted to Islam, he was known locally as Pakistani, even though he was born in Somalia, had never left Somalia, had never set foot in Pakistan. No matter how Raj and a few influential Somalis tried, the Somali government officials with power to grant citizenship refused to do so for Azad. To them, non-Somali shopkeepers would always be outsiders.

Finally, the Indian Embassy in Mogadiscio issued Azad a passport on the grounds that his mother's village had still been part of India when she was born and that her son was a minor. He carried an Indian passport without ever having been in India.

In later years, Azad went to the Somali Embassy in Washington, D.C. and tried to become a Somali citizen. Again, they treated him less than politely and refused him. He had dreamed of returning to Mogadiscio, of using his considerable skills in computer technology and everything he had learned for the benefit of what he still considered his homeland, but the Somali sense of clan-based identity remained strong.

How would we prepare this new member of our family for his life with us? When Azad's father decided that his son could live with us in America, I began thinking of small things the child would need to know if he were to adjust easily to American life. He began having dinner with us, American style, sitting at a table and using a knife, fork and spoon. I discovered that one of the new hotels in Mogadiscio had an elevator, so I took him and we rode up and down several times. He was frightened at first, but the second time we went up his eyes shone with the fun of it.

We included Azad in our family's favorite weekend afternoon entertainment: visiting Mogadiscio's airport. Raj drove the Fiat and I sat up front with him. Azad sat in the back seat, crammed between our son and daughter, stopping them from hitting one another, joking, teasing, diffusing the taunts they threw back and forth. I liked seeing the three of them together.

The airport building consisted of one large room with dark green louvered panel walls. Tall, thin, sometimes elegant

Somali men lounged, thoroughly at ease, on wood frame and rope chairs grouped around low wooden tables. They spent their time smoking, holding the cigarette between the front teeth, drinking sweet orange soda and arguing vigorously about Mogadiscio politics. Above, a whirring fan barely stirred the air. Standing about were Somali men in the traditional white cotton pillbox hat, white shirt, hosgunti (sarong) and sandals. Other Somalis, and men of at least a dozen nationalities, were dressed in suit, shirt and tie or slacks and open-necked shirt or a tropical outfit of a tailored short-sleeved shirt and matching trousers. A number of Arab men wore the dishdasha and turbans. An occasional mullah from the Al Azhar mosque of Cairo, distinguishable by his smart gray cloak and gray turban, stood alone, keeping his own austere company. Somali and Sudanese women looked dignified in their robes of a gracefully draped length of cotton cloth and a long shawl over the head and around the shoulders. Indian women looked splendid in bright silk saris and lots of gold jewelry. European women managed to appear chic, even in the tropical heat. The typical American woman's style was to be neat and casual. I delighted in watching everyone; I thought we all looked like extras on a movie set and half-expected Humphrey Bogart and Peter Lori to walk in and perform. After its inevitable modernization the airport became ordinary and I have quite forgotten how it looked.

In August, Raj bought tickets on Aden Airways for the first lap of our outbound journey and sold his funny little Fiat, cheap, to an Indian. I said my farewells to Zeynab and the girls and reassured them as best I could that Azad would be safe in our home and in school. We closed the house. I divided our furniture and kitchen equipment between Asha and Ahmed and introduced them as good and reliable servants to a newly arrived American family. I packed the clothes and souvenirs we would take home with us. Azad's father had new clothes made for him by a tailor in Hamar Wein and bought him a suitcase for his travels.

We flew from Mogadiscio's airport, as originally intended, as a family of five, all returning to school as teachers or students. For Azad and for me, in our imaginations we never left Mogadiscio but in reality we did leave and after 1991 there is no returning. Thugs calling themselves clan chieftains staged their power plays and vendettas on the streets of Mogadiscio, mindlessly destroying in days the physical and social structures that took generations, even centuries, to build.

Azad's family and his community eventually settled in other East African countries. Without breaking ties with his parents and brother and sisters, Azad went on to a life with us, his second family, in the United States and Europe.

But that is another story.

MY WOUNDED ANGEL

Over fifty years have gone by and I still puzzle over why I was so drawn to Malayko and so eager to help her. I marvel at the unlikely circumstances of our meeting and at our peculiar friendship.

It could have happened, of course, only in the 1960s, only during that brief era after independence when peace and civility reigned in Mogadiscio for everyone. It was a time when opportunities for a better life were open and plentiful, when a girl like Malayko, given the right circumstances, could blossom and prosper.

It was the autumn of 1966. Raj and I had arrived in Mogadiscio for our second stay in the city, again on research but this time with a more generous grant. We were still "on the economy" with no one in an Embassy or United Nations office to look after us and no pre-arranged social network. Somali friends helped us locate a place to rent, a proper house in a good compound, one of the hundreds of such houses being built to accommodate the foreigners swarming into Mogadiscio for Somalia's many and varied development programs. Our house had, as most Americans would expect, a kitchen with imported cabinets, a sink and running water, a small stove fueled with a propane gas "bomb" and an electric refrigerator. The bathroom was similar, if less well equipped, to one we would have had back home. The bedrooms and the living room/dining room were small but adequate and we furnished them with things made locally or with pieces bought from foreigners ending their tour of duty and moving on. I was reasonably competent this time to shop, cook, keep house in this simplest of economies and felt my burden considerably lightened when the guard and the servant woman, Ahmed and Asha, from our first stay in Mogadiscio heard we were in town and returned to us. Raj began his research. Our children attended the American school maintained by our Embassy, and they made friends to keep them happy. The school also accepted Azad, the boy from Mogadiscio whom we had taken into our family two years earlier. Once settled in, Raj and I soon made friends in the various expatriate circles -- American, Indian, European and British -- and they invited us to their parties and informal events. Having a social life among Somalis was another matter. Local people entertained mostly among close friends and with family, excluding outsiders, but we did learn of one place where a number of Somali men we knew spent their weekend evenings into the night. It was a nightclub, the Lido, located on the outer margins of the city, on the beach.

Raj and I decided to try the Lido for ourselves, so we dressed up, tucked the children into bed, well looked after by Ahmed, and stepped forth as a young couple to have fun, to become regular habitués of the Lido.

At the Lido, we talked and danced and inadvertently entered into a world where a respectable woman rarely ventured. Nor would a family man venture there if he were, like most foreigners, attached to an Embassy or development program and living in Mogadiscio with his wife and children. However, for Somali men, particularly the affluent senior civil servants and businessmen, and for single, foot-loose foreign men seeking nighttime pleasures, the demimonde we discovered was a normal feature in the social landscape.

The Lido was built in the 1930s as a beach club for Italians colonials, luxurious and well appointed, as were all buildings in the Italian Mogadiscio. However, entering the Lido in the 1960s and only at night I saw it merely as large, long and raw. A dance floor divided the nightclub into two areas, each with ten or twelve wooden tables and each table circled by as many chairs as could be crowded around it. Along the back wall ranged a bandstand occupied by a small group of Somali musicians playing dance music, mostly popular Italian tunes. One song lingers still, "Di mi, quando, quando, quando?" as does the sweet sound of Somali poems sung late, after the dancing ended, by a young Yemeni fellow who accompanied himself on a Sudanese lute. In a far corner a small, dark man I never saw up close stood behind a bar, dispensing drinks and cigarettes to the waiter who served our table.

After the Lido, we moved on to a candle-lit garden restaurant, also near the ocean, for a midnight dinner of pasta in a garlicky tomato sauce, sitting under the brilliant stars of a desert sky, surrounded by tropical greenery, refreshed by cool breezes. Sometimes Raj and I walked by moonlight to the shore. I liked to splash barefoot in the waves, move among mysterious florescent dots that floated in the water and try, always in vain, to catch and hold them.

At first I imagined our Saturday nights as reasonably like those in the nightclubs back home where we sometimes went with friends, but in the Lido it soon dawned on me that Raj and I were the only married couple. He and I sat on one end of the hall with our friends, all men. Across the dance floor were the women clientele, barely visible through the dim light and smoky haze. They sat clustered together, seemingly good companions enjoying themselves. I was the only White woman and the only woman who both began and ended the evening seated at a table in the men's section.

I knew something of the local customs; except for the foreigners or at events hosted by foreigners, in Mogadiscio men and women spent their leisure time separately and they entertained separately. It was true of the Somalis, the Indians and the Arabs. The house was for women, children and family affairs; women entertained other women at home. Men spent their leisure time in the cafés, in restaurants, at the cinema, going for long walks, and they socialized with other men. This was the first time I had seen women together in a public place. As the evening wore on and I watched one after another move on to the dance floor or join the men at our table, I realized they were in the Lido not for an evening out with the girls. They were there to sell their services.

For hours at the Lido, Raj and I, eager to understand everything about Somalia, discussed politics and public affairs with men who occupied top positions in the country's government. Young men, boys really, sat with us for a while, hovered around us, being friendly, waiting for us to share our table's bottle of whiskey or wine with them. By the band's second set they were crossing the room, circling the women's tables, taking one woman after another for a turn around the dance floor. Gradually the boys drifted back, bringing chairs to sit behind us.

The women, having displayed their charms on the dance floor, had dismissed the boys and turned their attentions to more substantial customers. When a man beckoned her, a woman walked across the dance floor divide to sit with him. Well before closing time a good many of the men had selected a woman for the night and left with her.

It took me awhile to arrive at an opinion about the prostitutes of Mogadiscio. Who was I to judge? When we lived in Mogadiscio in the early '60s, I had been most involved with the local Muslim Indian community and had not learned as much as I should have about Somali culture. I had missed, for example, informing myself about this large category of women who shared in the lives of Somali and foreign men. All I heard was that European men coming to Somalia went wild for the beautiful women.

I could not tell, just by looking, a prostitute from a respectable woman. They looked no different to me, or to any other foreigner. Most were tall, fine featured, with wavy hair. Nefretiti (without her headdress) would not have been conspicuous on the streets of Mogadiscio. Since I had picked up Italian, rather than the exceedingly difficult Somali, for ordinary conversation, I could not catch the nuances of accent, grammar, vocabulary that distinguished one sort of person from another. A Somali told me that most prostitutes came from the three outcast lineages of Somali pastoral nomadic society, the potters, leather workers and ironsmiths, but I

52

wonder. They were in every way an underprivileged and exploited minority. His remark could have been a perception from prejudice rather than fact.

The evening I met Malayko, Raj and I were at our usual table in the Lido. Several women had moved in among us and I could no longer follow the conversation as it turned to rather raucous joking and into Somali rather than Italian. I had no one to talk with and Raj did not want to dance. I sat fretting, wondering how I could quietly exit and go home, when a small hand took mine. Someone had slipped in to the chair beside me. I looked up to find a beautiful girl, sixteen or seventeen years old, tall and shapely, large round eyes and brown hair coiffed into ringlets.

She spoke in Italian. "Are you American?"

"Yes. What is your name?"

"Malayko"

"What a pretty name. It is Arabic for Angel, isn't it?"

I was prepared to ask her the questions I usually asked a young person, questions about where she lives, her brothers and sisters, where her father works, does her mother work, where she goes to school, her favorite subject in school, her best friend. I began with, "Where are your mother and father from?" meaning, in that context, her clan. In the United States, I would have first asked her father's occupation to locate her in the larger scheme of our society. In Somalia, knowing a person's clan and sub-clan gave basic information, about whether he or she is a pastoral nomad, northerner or southerner, village farmer, or from one of the coastal cities and this, in turn, gave clues to the person's social and cultural background.

"My mother is sitting over there." Malayko pointed across the room. I did not ask about her father. From the lovely golden color of her skin, a mixture of African and

Mediterranean, I inferred he was Italian. She did not mention other family so I let that drop as well.

A person without a legitimate father had no place in Somalia's patrilineal, patriarchal society. One belonged to the father's clan, sub-clan, lineage, family. Even at marriage, a girl did not change from her father's lineage to her husband's. Lineage determined a person's primary identity, gave shape to most aspects of his or her life, was the source of security, of protection. For the few Somalis I knew with a Somali father and European mother, life was good. They had the advantages of lineage, speaking English or Italian and a general appearance from the racial mixture that anyone will find attractive. Malayko had the language and good looks, in abundance, but she lacked a lineage. Hers was the status of a pariah. She was marked.

Malayko did not even belong to the one small community of mixed parentage, the Missioni. Although she was racially mixed, as were they, she was not socially acceptable to them.

The Missioni community was an inevitable outcome of Italian colonialism. From the early 20th century onward Italian administrators, missionaries and settlers came to live in or near Mogadiscio, and inevitably, Italian men fathered children by Somali women. Almost as inevitably, the man walked or sailed away from both the woman and his offspring, leaving them in an impossible situation; neither Somalis nor Italians would accept such a child into their fold. For the ill-fated woman, her only recourse was an orphanage, the Mission, where Italian nuns raised and educated abandoned children.

In the Mission compound nuns of the Cathedral sheltered the mixed race children against a world that scorned them. The Missioni children, as they were called, lived together and were schooled together. They stepped outside the Mission walls only in groups, closely supervised and protected by the nuns. From all I heard the nuns treated them kindly.

54

As Missioni individuals became adults, they married one another and had children who, in turn, married among their own kind, as would be expected by the larger society. A small Mogadiscio Missioni community evolved and acquired an ambiguous social status, accepted in neither Italian nor Somali inner circles of family and social life but recognized as essentially respectable and useful as employees within the local government and businesses.

The Missioni kept the Italian names the nuns had given them and they gave their children Italian names. They remained Catholic, as the nuns had taught them, and that further set them apart from the Muslim Somali nation. Missioni women, unlike most Somali women in those years, wore dresses, shoes and hairstyles in the same mode as those of the Italian and other foreign women. Naturally, both men and women spoke excellent Italian and many learned Somali as well. At a time when few Somalis were even literate, Missioni children were educated through secondary school. The men held clerical and business administrative positions. Girls worked as secretaries and the prettier ones mixed among wealthy Somali men as party girls until the time came for them to marry a Missioni man.

For the Missioni, a Somali woman who lived as a prostitute was beyond the pale and her mixed race daughter was socially unacceptable.

I said to Malayko, in Italian, "Tell me about school."

"I go to the Italian high school. Mama told them they had to take me in."

"And? Do you like school?"

"I kind of like it. But my teachers aren't nice to me."

"And? Who is your best friend at school?"

"I do not know any of the other students."

"Why not?"

"I stay up late at night with Mama so I guess I sleep in class. If I am not careful they will throw me out."

Malayko sat holding my hand until we left. She told me she had seen a postcard with the picture of a big statue of a lady on an island, so I told her about the Statue of Liberty. She listened raptly to everything I said to her, as if hungry for attention.

As Raj and I were leaving she asked, "May I come to see you after school tomorrow?"

I said, "Of course. Bring your books. I will help you with your homework."

When Malayko came to our house the next day she had already changed from her school uniform into a dress, one in the latest European fashion, with a mid-thigh length skirt. The Peace Corps women volunteers in Mogadiscio were wearing the same style, so I would not have given it more than a moment's thought, except that short skirts were definitely unsuitable in Somalia. Somali women wore either a dress with a long skirt or the traditional garessa, a five meters length of boldly patterned soft cotton cloth wrapped so that it fell from the left shoulder over the breasts and around the lower body to form an ankle length skirt. I often wore a garessa in the house because it was cool and comfortable. A woman's arms need not be covered and if a breast might occasionally be seen that was all right, too, but showing the upper leg in public was provocative, improper.

Malayko neglected to bring her schoolbooks the first day. I insisted, so when she came the next day and during the following weeks, we sat together at the dining table and reviewed her lessons. She made no effort to talk with my children. Azad, a teenager at that time, would not look at her. Our son and daughter regarded her simply as another of the many people who came and went in our home. They greeted her politely and carried on with their own activities.

On the third day she asked, "Do you like me?"

"Of course I like you. You are a nice person. You are intelligent, so it is easy to help you with your schoolwork. Why should I not like you?"

"Oh, it is only a question. You are nice to me. Why are you nice to me?"

At this point, I hesitated. My Italian was better for listening than for explaining the complex ideas going through my mind. "Perhaps I am nice to you because of things that happened to me when I was a girl. Like you, I had no family. My mother left when I was a baby and my father was not a good man. He fed me and gave me a place to live, but he was nasty. And he left me when I was younger than the age you are now. But I was lucky. A woman I called Grandmother took care of me. Teachers spent time with me. A woman in my church involved me in a young people's group and she took me to church parties with her. Neighbor ladies were kind to me. I do not remember their names but I remember all the nice things they did for me, like talking with me."

"Are all Americans good people like that?"

"Every country has good people and bad people. The problem in Somalia is most people are too poor to help someone who is not from family. But things are better now in Mogadiscio. I am certain if you study hard and your teachers see how well you do, they will help you. You will get lucky like I did and grow up to be happy. Now, tell me about school. What happened today? Did you recite in any of your classes? Did you talk with any of the other kids?"

"No. I am sorry. School does not please me."

Having failed to persuade her to talk about school I asked how she spent her time when not in school. "Mama watches the men playing cards and I stay with her." Her mother frequented a bar and made herself available to old Italian residents and rich Somali men who gambled together in the late afternoons.

"Do you have friends?"

"No. Just Mama's friends."

"Do you go to cathedral on Sundays? You could meet your school mates and teachers there."

"I do not want to be Catholic. I am Muslim, like Mama."

"Which mosque do you go to for prayer on Friday?"

"I do not know any of the mosques. Mama never goes there."

One evening at the Lido, before Malayko had crossed the room to talk with me, an American joined us at our table. I spoke sharply to him. "I've been watching you. Stop putting the make on that girl. There are plenty of women here you can buy. Let her be."

He laughed. "What do you think she is? She's already on her way and her mother's going to do pretty good off it, too."

He stood up, still amused, and walked away. A minute later Malayko was sitting beside me, very much a child, holding my hand.

Malayko had been coming to the house nearly every day for about two weeks when, one afternoon, when all the children were in school, her mother came to visit, walking unsteadily from the compound gate, down the driveway, past a disdainful Asha. She was a tall, with dark, clear, smooth skin and the Somali aquiline features everyone found so attractive. The garessa she wore draped nicely over her full breasts, small waist and rounded hips. I invited her to sit with me on the verandah and she slumped into a chair. When I handed her a cup of tea I could smell wine on her breath. She told me, slightly slurring her sentences, a tale about an Italian man who had promised to marry her and did not and how difficult her life was. She wanted money, so I gave her a small sum, to pay her rent. I discovered that she and Malayko lived in two rooms, in Shengani, an area of the city I knew. Mogadiscio had no red light district. She let me know that I had given her far less than she expected from her daughter's patroness, then stood up suddenly and left without waiting for me to walk her to the gate.

A Somali friend heard of the incident and said that certain men had warned her not to bother me again.

He added, "Missioni girls may come to your home, but not a prostitute." I had to agree that the mother's presence would seriously disturb my family and my household.

I did not speak with Malayko about her mother. What does one say to a child about her parents?

I did ask Malayko about her afternoons at the bar. "Do you enjoy them? Can't you stay away and spend more time with people your own age?"

She lowered her eyes. "I do not like Mama's friends. I will try to be good."

I wondered what more I could do for Malayko. I saw school as her only way out and up. At the least, with a high school diploma she could easily find a secretarial position. I could teach her English and that would further improve both her job prospects and opportunities for meeting people who would respect her as person. I had to help her overcome her dislike of school, persuade her to apply herself and please her teachers, help her face the disconnect between the world of school and her mother's world.

Each day I pushed Malayko to finish her schoolwork and each day she asked me question after question about life in America. Occasionally, to bring a smile to her pretty face, I translated into my simple Italian passages from my children's American social studies books. She forgot nothing I told her and was acquiring a fair English vocabulary. She learned easily, but she would not apply herself to the lessons assigned by her teachers.

One day, as I sat beside her, pencil in hand, again reminding her that school is important, she shrugged her shoulders at me and rose from her chair. She sauntered to the sofa and lowered herself slowly into the cushions, stretching her long shapely legs, watching the boys with a most unchildlike gaze. Azad struggled over his math book and graph paper, trying to concentrate. He squirmed and fidgeted. Our son, ten years old, had half the volumes of our World Book Encyclopedia set spread out on the floor. He began picking up one after another and, without reading, nervously flipped through the pages. Our daughter, eight years old, pretending not to notice, went to her bedroom, taking her book with her.

Raj took me aside. He spoke calmly but forcefully, in French, so the children would not understand. "The girl is upsetting the kids, and me. Do something about her." I think Malayko understand the meaning of what he said.

I heard talk that Malayko had become a fixture at the card games and a prominent man had taken her as his personal favorite. I had no right to ask her if it were true. Raj and I could not provide her with an alternative life; we had already assumed responsibility for Azad, as if he were our own son. We were carrying as much as we could handle, both financially and in dealing with three considerably different cultural backgrounds in one family.

Finally, I said to Malayko, "You must get serious with your studies. I cannot take more time away from helping my children with their school work if you do not apply yourself."

She repeated, "School does not please me." She added, "Mama wants me to forget it. I will be busy tomorrow."

She did not return. I could not go in search of her unless I had something positive to offer her.

Raj and I stopped going to the Lido. I had made friends among more traditional Somalis in the old *quartier* of Mogadiscio, families who would never approve of the Lido. As a couple, we became increasingly involved with an international set, exchanging dinners and parties in our homes.

Months went by. Our old Lido companions insisted they missed us, so Raj and I set aside a Saturday night for them and for sitting at our usual table. Once there, I avoided looking across the room, through the haze to the other side, for fear of whom I might see. I could not go onto the dance floor, where I would be especially conspicuous and scrutinized by the women. Instead, I turned my full attention to our friends' lively, always clever, banter. To my great annoyance, they were saying nothing new, nothing I had not already heard and thought about. I remarked on this to Raj and he agreed; we had already covered that territory. I sat for some time observing, now through eyes familiar with the scene, the self-satisfied men, the boys desperately seeking a patron and even more desperate women living in self-delusion. The novelty and mystery of the Lido were gone.

It was our last evening at the nightclub. We had better ways to spend our time. Besides, I did not want to be reminded. What could be Malayko's future? I had failed to rescue a sweet and beautiful child from the fate her society assigned her. My meager resources came to her too late. I stood by helplessly as she slipped away from me and from my world, across a social chasm into her mother's demimonde. I have no idea what happened to her.

AT THE YEMENI ALIMENTARI

Katherine was halfway between the verandah of her house and the gate of the compound wall when she remembered the string bag and returned to retrieve it from a kitchen cabinet. She leaned around the living room door, again waved goodbye to the children.

"Behave yourselves and I'll bring cookies for you from the grocery store."

She turned to Asha, speaking in Italian, "I will buy biscuits at the alimentari. We need rice and detergent. Anything else? Please fix chocolate milk for the children. I will be back in about an hour to begin dinner."

Asha held her broom still and replied, *"Bene, Signora."*

Katherine closed the gate behind her. She hurried past Mogadiscio's newly constructed, over-sized, over-capacity and still unused printing press, foreign aid from the Soviet Union for the newly independent Somalia, and turned from the dirt road onto one of the city's paved and tree-lined main streets. She walked past houses, through a piazza, past Italian stores, a café and a restaurant, turned left at the corner between the Banco di Napoli and Banco di Roma, passed the Cinema Nazionale, turned right onto the Corso Primo Luglio at the corner marked by a small ancient mosque. Her pace quickened as she passed the Café Nazionale, a large white building with a high room-wide arcade for billiards and café tables where young Somali men sat and argued politics. Then she paused to sit for a moment on a marble bench and quietly enjoy the view. Here the gray stone Cathedral, modeled after a church near Palermo, and the Governor's Palace, bright white, grandly Italianate, faced one another across the street. Their courtyards, filled with palm trees, trimmed hedges and flowerbeds, together formed a cool and pleasant open space within the heart of the city. She rose and continued walking, passed the Hotel Croce del Sud, turned left, passed the Cinema Centrale and arrived at her favorite road, the Via Roma.

Via Roma was paved, with sidewalks, tree-shaded and lined with whitewashed buildings that housed small shops where Indian shopkeepers sold cloth and clothing, shoes and sandals, toys and trinkets, all sorts of household goods. The owners and their families lived, along with two or three Italian families, in the buildings' second and third story apartments. Pathways between the buildings opened into the old city, the casbah, Hamar Wein.

It was late afternoon. Cool fresh air, flowing in from the ocean, lifted the torpor of midday heat. Siesta was over and shops were opening. Thin charcoal smoke floated outward from the crowded warrens of Hamar Wein as women began preparing the evening meal. Street traffic began moving, mostly the Fiat 1100 taxis and three-wheeled auto rickshaws. Somali men sauntered amicably, engrossed in conversation.

As she walked, Katherine looked into the shops, ready to wave to the men she knew. She depended upon these shops for items to equip her kitchen. For olive oil, cheeses and sandwich materials she went to an Italian deli and for bread to an Italian bakery. When her husband drove her to the Italian stores and restaurants and parked the car, boys from the street, "watch boys," swarmed around them, insisting she give them coins to watch the car. Unlike most Americans she knew, she did not frequent the Italian stores that sold high-priced, fashionable leather goods and clothing. Foreign women particularly valued bracelets made of ivory. They ventured also into Hamar Wein for the gold market where Indian craftsmen wrought jewelry in 24-carat gold and priced the brooches, bracelets, earrings and necklaces not by style but by weight.

Katherine arrived at the alimentari in time to see its owner, a man from Yemen, arrive at his shop. He was dressed in the typical Mogadiscio male attire: short-sleeved, open-necked white shirt; hosgunti, a meter-wide length of cotton cloth wrapped as a skirt; rubber thong sandals; white cloth pillbox hat. He also wore a wide belt in which he kept a key. He unlocked the shop door, swung it open and stepped behind the counter that stretched across the shop. Behind him, on the back wall from floor to ceiling, were shelves filled with canned and dry goods.

The Yemeni's customers were Italian colonials, foreigners and the relatively few Somalis who could afford to live in the modern economy. An Indian friend, the wife of an engineer with a company exploring for oil, had introduced Katherine to the alimentari. Most Americans and the U.N. personnel used their PX and import privileges for everyday needs and shopped in the Italian stores for luxury items. The average Somali bought at stalls in open marketplaces or from street vendors, and they bought in small amounts: tomato paste by the spoonful from an open can, a paper cone of rice or pasta, one cigarette at a time. Katherine purchased according to the needs of an American household: a can of tomato paste; cooking oil; biscuits; Danish powered whole milk; basmati rice; flour; corn meal; pasta; the Italian detergent, Omo. Wherever she shopped on Via Roma or in Hamar Wein, she usually stayed on for a few minutes, or longer, to chat with the man behind the counter, listening to stories he had to tell. The Indian shopkeepers spoke fluent English. The men from Yemen spoke Somali, Arabic and Italian. She had abandoned Somali as too difficult to pursue in the few years her husband would be working in Somalia, but her Italian was gradually improving and she practiced it at the Italian pharmacy and the Yemeni alimentari.

Each time at the alimentari Katherine asked the owner questions about himself and he answered freely. She suspected her accent amused him and often, when a word she used or the odd way she phrased a thought surprised him, he cheerfully corrected her.

He explained, "I was born in Sana'a. It is a great city but my family is poor. I went to the coast and took to the sea. I liked Mogadiscio, so I stayed. My wife is Somali. Sometime you come and visit us in Villagio Arabo, like you visit the Indians in Hamar Wein. Meet my wife and children."

He had come to Somalia by the same route as thousands of other Arab men, as sailors on the dhows, small ships that for millennia had plied the Arabian and East Africa coasts. They dropped anchor in Mogadiscio to buy and sell and barter and some stayed on to marry Somali women. One day, while wandering about the lovely old harbor, long since abandoned, Katherine had seen a dhow and recognized it as such by the long, sharp bow and triangular sail. An Arab sailor, barefoot, deeply tanned, bearded and shabbily dressed in dishdasha and turban, was walking toward the city, across what had been in a previous century the garden of a splendid house. A friend had told her that Arab sailors from various ports in the Persian Gulf came regularly into Hamar Wein. He said that as the men walked through the streets boys shouted "Basuri, Basuri" (man from Basra) and ran and hid; they had been warned that sailors kidnapped boys to work as slaves on the dhows. When Katherine told the alimentari shopkeeper about the sailor she had seen he told her that the ship's cargo would have been dates, raisins, dried fruits and nuts. In Aden, the old British port city in Yemen, south of Saudi Arabia, the sailors picked up watches and other small, high value items for smuggling. They sold and traded in the cities along the coast, first in Mogadiscio, on to Mombassa and Zanzibar, and down to Sofala in Mozambique. The sailor was sailing the monsoon, so for months he anchored his ship in Sofala, waiting for the winds to reverse and carry him home.

Katherine stood patiently as the shopkeeper swept the shop floor and rearranged boxes on the lower shelves. She was early and the only customer. A number of Somali men stood at the shop entrance, watching her. She recognized the older man from having seen him several times in Hamar Wein. She smiled a quick "hello" to him. The others were younger, in their early twenties, with one looking to be from the Hadhramaut Arab community and three with the features and build of a pastoral nomad. They had stopped for each to buy a cigarette from a street vendor next to the alimentari. The Arab wore slacks, shirt and shoes. The others were dressed in the same manner as the shopkeeper.

The four young men were laughing and talking, making remarks in Somali Katherine was certain were salacious. She tried not to notice, but when the older man spoke sharply to them and motioned them back so she could step to the counter, she thanked him. She took her coin purse from the string bag, asked the shopkeeper if Indian rice were available today and said she would take half a kilo, pointed to a can of powdered milk, a box of Italian detergent and a package of biscuits the children liked. She thought for a moment and said in Italian, "That is all for today. How much?"

She counted out bills and coins in Somali shillings, placed them on the counter, fit her packages into the bag, turned to leave and came to a sudden stop. She blurted out, in English, "Ohmygawd, who are you?"

Katherine found herself standing directly in front of a tall, thin Somali pastoral nomad. He was leaning on a long staff held in his right hand and did not move to let her pass by him. He was staring at everything around him, apparently transfixed, and seemed especially curious about this foreign woman.

The curiosity was mutual. Katherine had seen men like him only once before, when on an adventure in the countryside. She had gone in a Fiat 2000 with three Somali friends and her eight-year-old son to a village along the river behind Mogadiscio. They had begun the journey on the colonial Strada Imperiali, the road from southern to northern Somalia, and after some twenty kilometers outside Mogadiscio, had turned off the road, driving across flat, sun-baked, scrub-covered land. She had suggested before leaving that they borrow a Land Rover or, at least, a jeep for such travel, but the Somalis dismissed this as unnecessary. Nevertheless, a tire had blown on the way to the village and the driver had replaced it with their one spare. On the return to the road, in late afternoon, a second tire blew. After a quick consultation among themselves, the Somalis had informed Katherine that they would have to remain seated in the automobile, no matter how crowded they felt. They could not walk to the road. Too many poisonous snakes were around. After dark, leopards and lions would be out hunting. Being city men, they carried no spear or knife or gun and, even if they had, would not have known how to use it. The decision reached was to proceed to the road on the wheel rim and wait for another car to come by and rescue them.

Katherine had pulled her son close to her and he whispered, "Mom, I'm okay." She smiled reassuringly at him. All conversation ceased.

They had driven slowly, alone with nature and their fears, and reached the road just before nightfall. Unexpectedly, at the exact spot where they arrived, they found a tea stand and a man sitting on a stool at a table under a shelter, boiling water on a small kerosene burner. The shelter was about seven feet tall, made of four thin tree trunks as poles held in place on the ground with large stones, holding up a roof covered with brush. To the side stood three men, looking much like the man now in front of Katherine. Surprised at seeing so many other human beings in such a landscape, Katherine had announced "It's like Time Square," and from then on that place on the road was known among Katherine's Somali friends as Times Square.

The pastoral nomads in the bush and the one facing Katherine in front of the shop wore a white cotton hosgunti, a leather belt, a large white cotton shawl and leather sandals. Each held a long sturdy stick, the primary tool used in herding camels. They sported the full, puffed hairstyle favored by nomadic pastoral men of the region, a coiffure achieved by working tree resin into the hair. To preserve its neat, helmet-like shape, the man slept with a small wooden headrest that served as a pillow and looked like diminutive sculpture. Similar headrests, made of gold, are found in the tombs of Egypt's Pharaohs.

Katherine stood at the alimentari counter, stock still in front of the tall stranger, her string bag of groceries dangling from her right hand, uncertain about where to step. The four young men had arranged themselves on either side of the nomad, forming a semi-circle around her. They were smoking their cigarettes, in no hurry to leave, watching her, each letting her know by the smart aleck smirk on his face that for her to slip away she would have to brush between two of them and they were waiting for her to decide which two.

The shopkeeper's voice, slightly raised, speaking Italian, cut through to her. She realized he was trying to defuse the situation and give her the means for a dignified exit. He said, "Signora, are you in a hurry? Last time you told me about your farms in America. I have another question. In America, do you pray every day at sunrise and sunset?"

She drew in a deep breath and turned toward him, pausing for a moment to mentally translate her thoughts into Italian. She said, matching his serious tone, "No, because in America the sun rises and sets at different times of the day at different times of the year, so that would not fit with the way we live."

The young men's expressions changed, their attention caught by what they sensed was an important conversation. The shopkeeper translated into Somali for them. They all looked astonished.

The older man had been standing behind the nomad. He moved forward and asked, "Why is the sun different in America than in Somalia?"

"Because you live at the Equator and America is very far north of the Equator." The Yemeni again translated for the men.

Blank stares. "What does that mean?"

She said, "It is complicated. I cannot explain in my poor Italian, especially without pictures to show you."

The shopkeeper pushed a blank sheet of grainy gray paper across the counter. The older man ran across the street to another shop, returned with a pencil and handed it to her.

The shopkeeper said, "Explain. You can make pictures for us. I will translate into Somali. Do not worry about your Italian. I understand what you say."

The nomad and the other men edged in closer and two passersby stopped to join the group.

Katherine set down her packages, picked up the pencil and prepared herself. At the time, having grown up in Midwestern Protestantism, the common origins of many Muslim and Christian traditions were unknown to her. She had neither heard nor read of the Canonical Hours, an ancient Jewish tradition continued in Roman Christianity, or of Catholic priests in earlier centuries praying eight times a day, including at sunrise and sunset, similar to the current Muslim practice of five times a day. All she knew was that the faithful in Mogadiscio were called to prayer by the muezzin's clear, melodious voice as it soared from a minaret at sunrise and sunset, and no one where she grew up ever rang a bell from the church tower, except on Sunday morning, to remind the devout of their religious obligations.

She was, however, prepared to explain why hours of the day and night differ from one latitude to the next. The Muslim Indian community of Mogadiscio had asked her to teach in the secular school they were trying to establish for their boys and she had accepted. To prepare lessons for her classes, she was learning many basics in science, including the reasons we have day and night and seasons and why these vary around the globe.

Katherine drew, scratched out and redrew the solar system and a round earth circling the sun in a year's time and the moon circling the earth. She explained that both the earth and the moon are like a ball. The older man learned over and asked, "Where is Somalia?"

Katherine drew a larger earth, with a line through the middle. "This is the equator and Africa." She sketched in the continent. "Somalia is like a triangle north of the equator, along the ocean. Kenya down here, Ethiopia up here."

She smiled at her Yemeni friend and added a roughly drawn Arabian peninsula. "Sana'a is here, inland in Yemen. The port you first sailed from would be about here, on the Gulf of Aden, where the Hadhramautis come from. And Mogadiscio is here, almost on the equator."

A young Somali interrupted. "Where is America?"

She drew another circle and speaking in easily translatable sentences, "On the other side of the earth and far north. This is the equator and this line is the Tropic of Cancer. America is up here. Oh, dear! I cannot draw very well. I wish I had a real map. But I can show you why Americans and Somalis pray at different times."

She drew the earth spinning on a tilted axis as it circled the sun, with the tilt resulting, everywhere except at the equator, in varying hours for the sun to rise and set. She explained that far north and far south of the equator, beyond the Tropic of Cancer and Tropic of Capricorn, the sun's rising and setting causes four seasons and due to the tilt, the hours of rising and setting change throughout the year. In the northern half of the earth, the sun rises latest and sets earliest in late December. The days are short and the temperature is very cold. In late June the opposite happens; the daylight hours are long and the temperature is as hot as in Mogadiscio.

71

"You know that in Somalia the sun rises and sets at just about the same hour all year round and you do not have seasons like in America."

The shopkeeper corrected her. "We have the monsoon from the west and that makes a difference during the year. And the moon? Do you not pay attention to the moon?"

"People who live near the ocean do, for the tides, but I live in the middle of America. It is a very big country and until recently I had not seen the ocean, or even a large lake."

The shopkeeper said, "We live by the moon. When I learned Italian I discovered that you have a Christian calendar different from the Hijri. You ignore the moon."

Katherine was surprised, "A Christian calendar? The Hijri?"

"We have twelve months and each month begins with the new moon. We see the crescent and we have a new month."

"So that's it! About two months ago an Indian friend came to stand on the road in front of my friend's compound to look for the moon. She lives on the hill above the National Assembly and he said he could see the sky better from there. He came one evening and did not see anything. He came the next evening and saw the new moon. He told us he would fast the next day."

The shopkeeper said, "He was watching for Ramadan, the month of fasting, to begin. At the next new moon he would celebrate Id al Fitri and end the fasting."

"You have twelve lunar months? That does not add up to a year."

"The Hijrah fits our life. It is shorter than your Christian calendar but that is not important."

"It is called the Gregorian calendar. Now that the government and the foreigners keep the Gregorian calendar, what will you do?"

"We will keep the Hijri for our religion. If we need your Christian calendar it is easy to find. No problem."

Katherine returned to her drawing of the earth tilted on it axis and the consequences for seasons and differing climates north and south of the Tropics. Helping the men imagine climates other than their own was beyond her; they had no experience with distant places and conditions, but she did her best and they patiently listened through the translation. She could not refer to books and magazines because so few were available. She realized the men probably watched European and American films in the local cinemas but she did not know what they had seen or how they perceived foreign images on the screen. The most popular films were made in India and set in fantasy landscapes.

Then she remembered the equinox. "I will tell you what happened to me in March. One morning, I walked out of my house, to visit a friend, but at the gate I turned around and went back. I gave up. It was too hot to move. I spent the day sitting in the shade."

When the shopkeeper translated, the older man added that the same happened with him and the young men murmured their agreement. It had been the spring equinox, March 21, when the sun hovers directly overhead. She drew the equinox, with the sun crossing the equator twice a year and the shopkeeper added information, for Katherine's enlightenment, about the stars and constellations in March and September. At the Somali translation, the nomad nodded vigorously and added names for the constellations. She thanked them for the information.

She was about to explain the solstices as she knew them but paused; it would be difficult. She thought about the far northern lands and ancient structures, such as Stonehenge, for marking the days of the solstices and wondered if these two dramatic points in the seasons were the reason Europeans defined the solar year as primary and phases of the moon as units within it, rather than the year being, as in the Islamic calendar, a cycle of lunar months. Reluctantly, she decided against adding this complication to the discussion.

Instead, she told the men how surprised she had been with their sunrise and sunset. They looked puzzled as she described America's dawn, how the sun lifts slowly from below the horizon, tinting the skyline in shades of red from scarlet to pink, transforming night-time dark into a pale blue light.

"I miss twilight at the end of the day. The sky takes on fantastic colors -- red, orange, purple. And the sun slides towards the horizon and it disappears ever so slowly. The light changes, too. It glows. For a few minutes before it fades away everything is beautiful." She sighed as a wave of nostalgia sweep over her.

"Dawn and twilight here are very brief because the sun's rays do not slant toward earth the way they do in the north; they are directly overhead. The sun rises and sets quickly. I think of the sun in Mogadiscio as a light that is turned on in the morning and off at night."

Katherine paused and looked up at the earnest expressions on the men's faces. They came out of the spell, conferred among themselves and spoke with the shopkeeper. He said to her, "Now we understand why our sunrise and the sunset prayer come always at the same hour year round. We can build our lives around them. We regret that in America you cannot pray as we do, but it is the will of Allah."

Katherine handed the pencil to him and said, "*Buona Sera.*"

The older man caught the shopkeeper's attention and asked for translation. He wanted Katherine to know that he would tell all these new ideas to his friends.

One of the young men spoke in halting Italian. "*Signora, molto grazie.*" Many thanks. She bowed a little, acknowledging their newly discovered good manners toward her.

To the nomad she said "*Nabad.*" Peace. He responded, "*Nabad gelyo*," Good-bye.

The crowd that had gathered dispersed.

Katherine picked up her groceries. She had to hurry home, for the sun would soon set and darkness would fall, like a light being turned off.

THE STREETS OF HAMAR WEIN

"Signora! Sheik Ali a venuto, a la porta principale!"

Katherine called after Asha, in Italian, "At the gate? Who is at the gate?"

Katherine's household, normally somnolent in Mogadiscio's midday heat, was suddenly aflutter with activity. Asha had run past Katherine, rushed to the kitchen and scolded the cook out of his lethargy. She shouted at him that the Signora had an important guest and get out a pan, get some water boiling. Katherine could hear them rummaging among the spice jars for cardamom to add to the tea leaves, dragging a chair to the cupboard to bring down the tin of imported biscuits she kept on the topmost shelf. Ahmed, the guard, was hurrying from his corner of the garden where he and his several cousin-brothers lazed away their afternoons. Katherine put down her magazine and went to the front door, arriving in time to see Ahmed's friends slip over a low place in the compound wall, undoubtedly on their way to inform everyone they knew about the momentous good fortune that had descended upon Ahmed's American family.

Ahmed came to Katherine's side, asking permission to open the gate for Sheik Ali.

"No. I will go myself. This noise will be waking the children and Signore Dan. He will need your help with them." Shifting from Italian to English, she said, to no one in particular, "Who in the world is Sheik Ali?"

Katherine walked down the driveway to the gate, lifted its rusty latch and pulled back the high, heavy metal doors. Six Somali men stood facing her. She knew, from their mode of dress, they were not from the modern elite sector of Mogadiscio society, where men assumed the international style of shirt, trousers, jacket, shoes and stockings. These men wore the typical urban Somali outfit: a short-sleeved, open-necked

77

white shirt worn over the hosgunti (sarong), rubber thong sandals, a traditional white cotton pillbox cap. The tall, handsome, somewhat portly man at their center was dressed in the same fashion, but his shirt was newer and whiter and the blues and reds of his hosgunti were still bright. Obviously, he was the great Sheik Ali. Katherine guessed from his copper toned skin color that the Sheik was from the prestigious lineage believed to be descended from men of Shiraz, the ancient Persian city. In the casbah, Hamar Wein, their lineage was called the Shanshia.

Behind Sheik Ali stood Nur, a young man Katherine had met the previous week. He stepped forward and greeted her in English, "Signora, the Sheik speaks Somali. No English. No Italian." She nodded and paused, searching for the right balance of deference and dignity, then addressed the central person in the assembly, "Sheik Ali, excuse me for not speaking Somali but Nur will translate for me. Our house is much honored by your visit. Will you not enter and accept our hospitality?"

Sheik Ali greeted her, "We come in peace." The men stepped into the compound and she lead them to the house, walking beside, rather than in front of, the Sheik, both to show respect and to better observe him. She thought him to be in his late thirties but trying to look older and weightier. He had shaved his head. His expression was composed, emotionless, and his demeanor was stately, deliberate. They crossed the verandah, into the living room and Katherine directed Sheik Ali to the center of the sofa. The other men arranged themselves around him, leaving space for the Sheik to reign over the conversation. Asha had tea ready, with the best teapot and the prettiest cups and saucers arranged on the coffee table. She stood at the kitchen door and watched as Katherine poured and served.

They waited. The Sheik spoke and Nur translated into Italian. "I hear that you want something impossible and you have been speaking about it with my people. They say you want the streets of the old city to be paved." He hesitated. "Do you think it can be done?"

Katherine said, "Perhaps. Times have changed. Since independence, many governments and agencies are interested in Somalia -- the U.N., Common Market, embassies. They might help. Who knows?"

Sheik Ali sipped his tea and tasted the shortbread as he listened to the translation. His expression softened a little. Nur translated in a mixture of English and Italian. "I hear about you. You and Sharif teach in the Indian school in their mosque. Do you know that Sharif is from Brava? He is a city man, like us in Hamar Wein. People say you and Sharif help the Indian boys learn English. The Sheik in the Jama Mosque told me he took you inside the mosque and you climbed to the top of the minaret. Do you know that the mosque is over 700 years old?"

"Yes. I know."

Sheik Ali's voice rose slightly. "Our grandfathers tell stories about what life was like before the Italians came. We were a good city, but the Italians wanted their own, much grander place. They took our name. Now their part of the city is called Mogadiscio. People call us Hamar Wein."

"Yes. I know. I have read about Mogadiscio before the Italians. I know about Ibn Battuta's diary, from when he visited Mogadiscio in the 1300s. He described the fine buildings. He wrote that the men were dressed in silken robes and they gave him dinners of lamb and rice pilaf and tropical fruits. Vasco de Gama landed in Mogadiscio. He would have set fire to the city, like he did others down the coast, but the trade winds blew him and his ship out to sea, just in time to save Mogadiscio. It would be wonderful to see Hamar Wein as fine as it used to be. I can imagine ..."

Katherine stopped and turned quickly to Nur, "That is too complicated. Just say that I know Mogadiscio is an old city and it was beautiful."

Sheik Ali listened, then rose slowly from the sofa. His companions leapt to their feet, hastily setting down cups and biscuits. "I would like for us to talk again next week, on Tuesday morning, after your class." Nur looked pleased as he translated. "If you agree, Nur will call for you and guide you to my home in Hamar Wein."

Katherine replied, in all sincerity, that she would be happy to meet with him. She noted that he knew her schedule, knew the hours, those when Dan was in his office and her children were in school, when she was free to move about in Hamar Wein and elsewhere, attending to her own interests. She walked with the men to the gate and bid them farewell, watching them as they strode onto the dusty road in front of her compound.

As she closed the gate Katherine searched her memory, reconstructing the events that had brought Sheik Ali and Nur to her house. The series of events began with her meeting Sharif at the Jama Mosque for him to take her to meet Nur and his women folk, then Nur coming to the house for her to give him an English lesson.

Katherine had been late that morning for her meeting with Sharif. A sudden rainfall, a torrential downpour, had come without warning, holding her on the verandah staring in wonder as water poured silvery off the roof, flooded the compound and vanished into the sandy soil. Somalis told her that when the sometimes-torrential rain arrives in the country-side gullies become instant rivers. A moving wall of water roars down a hollow, lifting and tumbling whatever lies in its path, traveling at such speed that a person can be caught and drowned, right there in the middle of a semi-desert. Then the rain stops as unexpectedly as it began. The river drops its cargo and melts into the land.

Because of a drainage system for city streets, monsoon rain caused little or no damage in Mogadiscio proper, but it did bring misery to Hamar Wein, where narrow streets and paths went unpaved and undrained, where donkeys, goats, cows, chickens dropped excrement and children tossed peelings and pits underfoot as they ate on the run. Normally people could tolerate the mess. They swept the dirt aside or let it be worked into the hard-packed street surface. A breeze moving in from the ocean freshened the air, and the sun penetrated between the two- and three-story buildings. It was when the skies opened and water fell as if from a great upturned caldron that walking in Hamar Wein became almost intolerable. The streets turned to mud and they smelled foul.

Sharif had been waiting patiently for Katherine. She greeted him with "Ah, my cicerone."

He laughed. "You use many words I do not know, but that is all right. You help me so I do not lose my English. Come. I want you to meet my friend."

They had walked into the alley-like streets of Hamar Wein, watching their feet, stepping cautiously from one small dry spot to the next. Katherine concentrated on shallow breathing to avoid the stench and said nothing except "Damn it!" once, when she barely missed slipping into a pool of filth. She waved her hands back and forth in front of her face to clear a space in the cloud of flies.

Children running along the street stopped, out of curiosity, to stare at Katherine and catch her attention. She said to Sharif, "These children have skin infections. They're coughing. Even the grown-ups get infections. These filthy streets make people sick."

Katherine admonished her friend, as if it were his fault, "Sharif, this should not be."

"What can be done? Hamar Wein is always a mess during the monsoon. It will go away in a week or so. Try covering your nose but watch your feet. I want you to meet Nur. He will be the first Shanshia you've met. He speaks Italian very well and now is taking English lessons, so he will ask you to help him speak better. He is a good fellow. You will like him."

Brushing away flies and stepping carefully, Katherine had followed Sharif to a large building in the center of Hamar Wein. They entered into a hallway, through a door with an intricately carved lintel to a white-walled room furnished with a table, low stools, a few straight backed chairs and a rope bed high enough for a storage trunk to fit underneath. Covering the bed was a white cotton sheet decorated with a border of red and green embroidered circles and squares.

Their host, Nur, said, in English, "I am pleased to meet you. Welcome."

Sharif moved a chair to the furthermost wall and remained there throughout their visit. Nur opened an inner door, leading three women, his mother, wife and sister, into the room to meet Katherine. Several children followed and sat on the floor. The women were dressed for the occasion, in new long dresses and hand embroidered headscarves of vivid pink sheer nylon, a fabric far more expensive than the usual cotton available in the Indian shops.

A bottled orange drink was served and the mother began the conversation. Nur translated. Names were exchanged. The age of each child was told. Katherine admired the wife's embroidery work, and the mother brought out a cap her daughter was crocheting for Nur to wear in the mosque. Katherine asked for information. Recently a family in Hamar Wein had presented her with an Italian-style cake that the women had baked. How could they possibly bake a cake when they have no stoves and cook over an open charcoal fire? Nur's mother explained that they use a tin oven that they place on a bed of glowing charcoal, cover the top with more coals, judge the internal heat and know, from experience, how long it takes for the batter to rise and cook.

The mother told Katherine that she sees her almost every day in Hamar Wein, and they all laughed when Katherine responded, "But I never saw you!"

"You didn't see me, except for my eyes. We Shanshia women are the ones covered in black cloth. The Indian women wear that cover they call a burqa."

When Katherine and Sharif bid their farewells and stepped outside, Nur went with them, guiding them through the shortest path out of Hamar Wein to the Lungo Mare, the ocean road. Sharif, with a teasing glance at Katherine, had said, "Nur, Signora Blake is shocked by Hamar Wein's dirty streets. What should we do about that?"

Katherine had protested, "It isn't just me. Everyone is miserable during the monsoon. Look at how sick the children are! These streets should be paved!"

The following morning Nur had come to the house. Katherine had seen Dan off to work, the children off to school and was preparing tea for herself. She asked Nur to join her at the dining room table. He asked, "Signora Blake, you said the streets in Hamar Wein can be paved. Is that true?"

"Maybe. What a project it would be! We would have to organize it. And find funding. But first things first. I brought home books from my children's school. Let's work on your English lesson. Please call me Katherine."

They read together from a fourth grade textbook and Nur learned several new words. After an hour he had bid her farewell and departed.

Now a week had passed and Katherine had not seen Nur again until this day, with Sheik Ali and the other four men. Questions whirled through her mind, the most persistent being how her servants knew about Sheik Ali. Ahmed was from a village farming clan. Asha was from a pastoral sub-clan in a region to the west of Mogadiscio. For both, Sheik Ali's ancient urban community had to be an unfamiliar world.

Katherine found Asha in the garden setting up a table, padding it well with towels and sheets, and preparing the charcoal iron. Asha preferred her own to Katherine's iron and, even though the charcoal sometimes spit out sparks that burned tiny holes in the family's clothing, Katherine let Asha carry on as she wished. Mogadiscio's electric supply was irregular, and given that it was produced by diesel fueled generators, outrageously expensive.

Katherine spoke in Italian. "Asha, how do you know about Sheik Ali?"

"Everyone knows about him. He is better than a doctor. Allah has given him the gift of healing, and he shares his gift with anyone who needs help. He can cure cancer and the evil eye and fevers, and he can drive out the devils when someone goes mad. He knows all of the Koran and can tell us what it means. He is a great man. And think of it! He came to your home and invited you to his home."

Asha paused, iron in hand. "Signora, the Italian part of Mogadiscio is so nice. Signora, why do you spend so much time in Hamar Wein? How did you even find it? All those narrow streets and old houses …"

"I started going there when an Indian man who works in Dan's office showed me the Indian shops and those men helped me rent this house and buy things. They all speak English. I spent a lot of time in their shops in Hamar Wein and Via Roma, and they asked me to teach in their school. You know Sharif, the teacher from Brava. He lives in Hamar Wein. The Indian men take me to meet their families, and they translate so that I can talk with the women. Of course, Hamar Wein women are not as free as other Somali women. I hate seeing women trapped in the veil.

"Still, I like Hamar Wein. It is a city and I grew up in a city. I know nothing about herding camels or about farming. I am used to buildings and people on streets."

Asha set to her ironing. "When I used to keep the sheep and goats with my mother the air smelled sweet and everything was clean. Hamar Wein is so dirty."

Katherine asked, "Is the rain finished?"

"Yes, Signora. I think we will have no more rain now until the monsoon. The big rains. Maybe six months."

That evening Katherine and Dan were invited to a party. He parked his Land Rover outside the Ambassador's compound wall, among the Fords and Chevrolets and they walked past several uniformed chauffeurs, all Somali, waiting relaxed and composed until their services were needed, some wearing woolen army coats against the cool night air. Once inside the large, well-furnished house set in its well-lighted and well-watered gardens, Katherine took a gin and tonic from the waiter's tray and looked around the room for the Director of the development agency responsible for assistance to projects in Somalia. She found him at the canapé table, not yet engaged in cocktail party small talk.

"Can you take a few minutes to talk about something with me?"

"Sure. What's happening?"

"Lots, for me, at least. I'm thinking of getting involved in paving the streets of Hamar Wein. Would the development agency pay for a project like that?"

"Boy, you really go where others fear to tread. At least other foreigners. Are you sure you want to get involved?

"I can't think of why I shouldn't."

The Director shook his head, "Then think about the development projects you've seen. Even the best ones fizzle. Even

85

most of the Peace Corps projects. And you are a complete outsider. It's a tricky business and pretty thankless, too."

"But I have friends in Hamar Wein. Today a whole group of men came to my house, and the one who seems like the leader talked about paving the streets. He looks like someone I can help get things done."

"Maybe, but I've seen projects start with a strong-minded person like you and fall apart because everyone comes from a different direction. There are always factions and they all work for what they want, even if it isn't what the project needs. Paving the streets is a good idea, but my guess is that your chances of pulling it off aren't all that great."

Katherine bristled. "If it is such a good idea, why don't you just have someone go in and do it? It wouldn't be expensive, at least compared with what most of the projects around here cost. The people are so poor. A few shopkeepers in Hamar Wein make a decent income by local standards, but even they couldn't afford to pay for all that cement and whatever else would be needed."

"No. We will not do it for them. Remember my telling you about a windmill I saw last year, for bringing up water from a well? Well, I've seen two more since, so I asked around about them. Windmills seem like a good idea in this kind of country. These were installed years ago by the Italians for the Somalis. And that's the problem. By outsiders for the Somalis. The Somalis never understood how the contraptions were put together or how they worked. The pastoral nomads haven't had much experience with machines, so maintenance and repair isn't something they think about. Now the windmills sit there, rusting into the ground."

He smiled at her. "I hear about you going out with your Somali friends to the villages. You told me once you were surprised when you saw farmers using small diesel pumps to irrigate their fields from the river. Did you know the farmers put those in themselves? They know everything about the pumps and they've kept them going all these years. Think about it. Even paving has to be maintained and repaired."

Katherine said, "You have never been in Hamar Wein during the monsoon. The few outsiders who go there at all only go in as far as the gold market to buy trinkets. Do you have any idea how bad those streets can be? I just can't see why people should live in such misery when the solution is so simple!"

"Okay, then, I'll tell you what. If you can organize this project and have someone credible in Hamar Wein take charge of it, the development agency will fund it."

"That's great. Believe me, I won't forget your advice. I will be very, very careful."

Katherine lay awake that night reflecting on the Director's words. Should she chance involving herself in a project that could easily go wrong? She enjoyed her life in Hamar Wein and people there accepted her, despite her being a fair-skinned, blue-eyed foreigner, because they knew her as a teacher. They accepted her moving about as freely as a man, but Sheik Ali might not be so tolerant. He had the air of a patriarch and a man accustomed to deference from everyone. Would he cooperate with a woman, especially one younger than he? To lull herself to sleep she repeated in her thoughts, like a mantra, "Go with the flow and all will be well. Go with the flow … …"

After her class on Monday morning Katherine walked with Sharif to the three-room apartment he and his wife rented in Hamar Wein. They were both from an ancient coastal city south of Mogadiscio, a community similar to Hamar Wein and even more conservative. The wife was young and pretty, with dark brown skin, a little plump, with curly hair and the large, round eyes most Somalis considered the height of beauty. Sharif was good-looking, trim and well built, with, like the Shanshia, a bronze skin color. He had trained as a teacher in London for nearly a year, was at ease with foreigners and understood Katherine's curiosity about everything around her.

Sharif's wife made tea and they sat together, with Sharif's infant son sitting bare-bottomed on his mother's lap and their four year old daughter leaning against Katherine.

Sharif said, "Katherine, everyone knows that Sheik Ali visited your house. That was an honor for you. People go to Sheik Ali; he does not go to them."

"Tell me about him. What is he like?"

"Well, everyone listens to him and they go to him for advice. There is no one else like that in Hamar Wein. He helps people. He speaks perfect Arabic, like someone from Cairo. And he is a Sheik."

"How does he make a living?"

"His family owns the building he lives in and he rents out part of it. And he knows how to heal sick people. He does not take money from a person, like the Italian doctors do, just for seeing a patient and talking, but when he gives someone herbal medicine or an amulet, I think that is the word, the person pays something for it, whatever he can afford. The Sheik probably makes some money there. And when he cures someone they always give him a gift to thank him. I have seen him get some pretty big gifts, money and things."

With the midday approaching, Katherine lifted the girl off her lap and said her goodbyes. She walked briskly through Hamar Wein, to the Italian Mogadiscio, to her house and garden. She wore, like a Somali woman, a light cotton shawl to cover her hair and pull over her face for protection from the wind and the dust. On arriving home, she went first to her bedroom to undress and shower in cold water. Waiting on the bed for her return was a brightly patterned five meter length of thin cotton cloth. Asha had taught her how to tie and wrap the cloth Somali style into a garessa, a light, comfortable dress draped over the breasts and shaped into an ankle length skirt, perfect for wearing at home.

The family lunched together, followed by each member of the household slipping into a quiet, near motionless state. After four o'clock, when the air had cooled to a tolerable temperature, they returned to their normal activities. Beyond their compound walls, shops and offices had reopened and the streets had returned to life. Nur and three other young Somali men came to visit. They practiced English and had tea and cookies with Katherine and the children.

On Tuesday, the day of her all-important meeting, after teaching her class, Katherine met Nur at Sharif's apartment. For half an hour she talked with Nur, tuning his ear to her accent, practicing a vocabulary he could easily understand, with no slang or colorful idioms. At 11:30 they left to walk to Sheik Ali's home.

The house they entered looked no different to Katherine than any other in Hamar Wein. In an upstairs room Sheik Ali received her, seated, with five women standing behind his chair. He invited Katherine to sit in a chair beside him. At a signal from the Sheik, Nur introduced Katherine to the women. The elderly matron was the Sheik's mother, the pretty young woman his wife, two were married sisters visiting their mother and one was a widowed aunt. The women listened, examined Katherine's face and avoided eye contact with Nur. They were not included in the discussion.

A servant brought a tray of sweet cardamom flavored tea, served in glasses. Sheik Ali asked and Nur, standing between them, translated, "Did you think again about paving our streets?"

Katherine said, "Yes, of course. But I have been thinking. Where in the government should we go to ask if it is okay. What is the government in Hamar Wein? Who is the mayor?"

"Government? Mayor? I hear Mogadiscio has a mayor."

"Do you elect anyone from Hamar Wein to go to the city government for you?"

Sheik Ali looked puzzled and raised his hand in a negative gesture.

Katherine continued. "We have four major clans in Hamar Wein, plus the Indians and a few Yemeni Arabs. Do the heads of these communities ever meet and decide together for Hamar Wein?"

"No. Why should they?"

"Hmmm. I'll have to think about this. Could we meet again in a few days?"

Katherine did not mention the development agency. She said only that they might receive money from some international organization.

As she took leave of the meeting Katherine paused in front of shelves holding a dozen or so leather bound books. Sheik Ali handed her one to open and admire. "They have been in the family for many, many years." The books were treasures passed from generation to generation, hand written in Arabic and decorated with gold, exquisite and rich, almost opulent objects, incongruous in their utterly simple setting.

For the next two days Katherine excused herself from all activities in Hamar Wein and abandoned any concern other than Thanksgiving. Dan stayed home from work on Wednesday to help with the preparations. She brought out cans of food saved for the occasion, cranberry sauce and pumpkin and candied yams. As the children watched wide-eyed, the cook beheaded the four hens Asha had been fattening in the back of the garden. All that day and Thursday morning Katherine and Dan and children worked to produce a genuine Thanksgiving dinner. Friends were invited to join them at the table. They feasted together and gave thanks.

Katherine's children were home all day on Friday and Sunday. The Americans had split the weekend in respect for the Muslim Sabbath and for Somalis who worked in the Embassy, the American school and their homes; Saturday, instead of Friday, became a work day. On Saturday afternoon Katherine met a Somali friend, a senator in the National Assembly, for coffee at the Croce del Sud café. She explained to him her concerns about government permission for a street-paving project. He said she needed to talk with the Mayor of Mogadiscio and this was as good a time as any to do so. From the café they turned onto Via Roma, walking behind the Governor's Palace on their left and shops on their right, past the Triumphal Arch to the Municipio, city hall, set in a manicured garden. They met the Mayor in his office. He cheerfully declared his approval of any project that would improve Hamar Wein. He said the streets were publicly owned and saw no problem with paving them, especially since it would cost the government nothing.

The Mayor promised to invite Sheik Ali to his office and settle with him all questions concerning rights to pave the streets of Hamar Wein.

Within days Nur arrived at Katherine's house with a message from Sheik Ali. She was being asked to meet with him in his home. Once there, Sheik Ali informed her that he and the Mayor of Mogadiscio had met. Together they had resolved all the questions posed by the municipal government. She was not to bother herself further about matters of legality and government sanction of their project.

Katherine responded by informing Sheik Ali that the development agency had agreed to support the project.

Katherine watched Sheik Ali as Nur translated what she had said about the development agency's procedures in such matters. As head of the project, Sheik Ali would have to make an appointment with the Director and apply personally for the funding. She thought the Sheik looked startled, but he had turned quickly toward his bookshelf, as if urgently in search of something, and when she could again see his face it held its customary benign, placid expression.

Katherine could not ask but she suspected the Sheik Ali rarely saw and had never spoken with the new genre of foreigner who had taken over Mogadiscio. He had known and dealt for years with the Italian colonials but after independence in 1960 everything changed. A large contingent of U.N. personnel and other foreigners arrived in Somalia to assist the new government in establishing Ministries and bureaucracies and because of the Cold War and Somalia's strategic location, Mogadiscio, with a population estimated at somewhere between 90,000 and 120,000, was host to 26 Embassies, each of which kept a full staff. Many supported at least one development program. Foreigners were ever present, but not in Hamar Wein and not in the daily life of men and women as traditional as Sheik Ali and his family.

The week went by without word from Sheik Ali. Nur visited Katherine to practice English. He said that Sheik Ali was occupied with religious matters and had not mentioned the paving project.

Saturday evening arrived and Katherine and Dan were invited for the usual weekend party with the Embassy set, this time at Nancy and Ted's well appointed home.

"Katherine, I've been waiting to hear from you." It was the Director. "What's happening with your project?"

"A snag. I have to figure out how to handle this. Would you mind going along with me on a rather unconventional way to set up an appointment? A young man working in your office is from Hamar Wein. Your secretary knows him. Would it be all right with you if she types out an invitation to Sheik Ali for an appointment with you and have this Hamar Wein kid deliver it? It would be nice if she could write it on good paper with your most impressive letterhead."

"Sure. Why not? I'll see that it goes out on Monday. Come, let's have a drink. Better yet, let's dance. Great music."

On the following Tuesday morning Nur was waiting for Katherine when she finished teaching her class. "Sheik Ali wants to see you now. Please come with me."

Sheik Ali announced, "I have an appointment with the Director of the development agency in his office. Will you come with me?"

"Of course. I will be delighted to be there with you when you explain the project and sign the paper. May I suggest that you take Nur as your interpreter. The development agency interpreter is from the north and may not be comfortable with the Hamar Wein dialect."

Sheik Ali, Nur and Katherine met the Director in his office. The Director said he had heard about a community street-paving project. Would Sheik Ali be leading the project? With the affirmative answer Sheik Ali and the Director discussed the project and decided they were still too early in the planning phase to talk specifics, but the Americans would supply or purchase all materials, including, but not limited to, cement and pipes, and all transportation of goods.

The following Saturday evening Katherine and Dan went to a party for the geologists who had just returned to Mogadiscio after weeks of camping in the bush. Dan warned Katherine that they were hell-bent on having a good time, with loud music on the phonograph, Somali girls and an ample supply of beer.

Katherine found herself in no mood for revelry. Instead of dancing or engaging in the usual banter, she sat alone, distracted. A young man from Dan's office sat down beside her. "You are off in the clouds. Something here on earth going wrong?"

"Ziad! You are exactly the person I need! You're a civil engineer, so tell me if I am in over my head. I'll explain. It's about a project to pave the streets of Hamar Wein. Maybe we've taken on more than we can handle.

"I'm working with an important man in Hamar Wein. He has the government's okay and the development agency will fund him, but we know from nothing about paving streets. The development agency's engineer has really big projects going. We are small time. How to handle the cement? How will drainage be done? What problems will we run into that haven't even occurred to us? Sheik Ali has never done anything like this, and it's certainly a first for me."

Ziad said, "Well, I can tell you right now that drainage will be no problem in Hamar Wein. It is an old settled area and lies higher than the surrounding city. Can you arrange for me to meet your Sheik Ali? You need to find out what is under the streets, things like electric wiring, sewage pipes and such. The older men will know. I'll speak Arabic with the Sheik. After all, it is my first language. How about tomorrow afternoon? I'll be in my office. Your friend can take me to Sheik Ali. His name is Nur? I'll be waiting for him."

Two days later, as she walked to her class, Katherine saw Ziad and Sheik Ali together, absorbed in conversation. She watched as they moved along the street, stopping, pointing, Ziad writing notes. They did not notice her. She continued on her way, feeling alone and isolated, an outsider in this Somali and Arabic world.

Once returned to her house Katherine waited, and as she expected, Nur soon arrived to announce that Sheik Ali wished to meet with her. They went together to his home. He was seated in his throne-chair, his women respectfully behind him. They listened attentively as he informed them that his good friend Ziad, an engineer and master of Arabic poetry, had reviewed with him the technical problems that might arise in paving the streets. They could all rest assured that the engineering aspect of the project would be exceedingly simple.

Katherine left the meeting feeling pleased with the project's progress but faintly annoyed that, again, no one had mentioned her contribution to solving its problems.

No one mentioned anything at all for quite a while; activities around the project came to a halt. Ramadan, the ninth month of the Islamic lunar calendar, had begun and Christmas fell some three weeks later. For Muslims, for a month, from one new moon to the next, from sunrise to sunset, the faithful must fast; when the sun is above the horizon they must abstain from food, drink, sex and tobacco. They were ill tempered during the day and totally engaged in feasting and festivities after sunset, late into the night. For the foreigners in Mogadiscio, the international holiday season, a time for family, entertaining and vacation began with Christmas and ended after New Year's Day.

On the day of celebration that ended Ramadan, Katherine offered sweets to Somali and Indian friends who came with their children to call on her and her family. Everyone was dressed in new clothes and feeling in a holiday spirit.

The next morning Nur arrived to say that Sheik Ali wanted to see her. He was ready to move on the project. In the meeting that afternoon, the Sheik announced to Katherine, Nur and his attentive women that he had decided which streets and open spaces were to be paved. Katherine listened, nodding in agreement, waiting to present an idea of her own. For weeks she had been developing and refining a plan that pleased her with its ingenuity, its simplicity and its potential for bringing the greatest good to the greatest number. When Sheik Ali finished speaking, she spoke. She laid her splendid plan before him.

Katherine reminded Sheik Ali that an abandoned lot lay alongside the mosque wall. She wanted something for the women. She proposed clearing the empty lot, surrounding it on all sides with a high wall, securing it with a strong door to protect the women inside, paving the space, piping in water through a hole in the mosque compound wall, and putting in drainage. A nice, clean place could be created for women to bathe and do laundry. They could have a toilet there, too. After all, the men have toilets in the mosques.

Sheik Ali stiffened and shifted uncomfortably in his chair. "It is not a good idea."

"Why not? Because it is for the women?"

"It is not a good idea."

"But Sheik Ali! That isn't fair!"

Nur used Italian for Sheik Ali's response, "*Bene.* It is as you wish. I went to a woman's house to begin this project. I did not wait for you to find me. It is now apparent whose project this truly is."

Katherine lowered her head, stared at her hands on her lap and sat still for a long moment, controlling the anger that swept through her. Words to scream at Sheik Ali raced through her mind, but finally they were "cool it." Should she try to persuade him? No. She was the outsider. She must concede or all they had accomplished together could be lost.

Nur was waiting apprehensively for her to give him something to translate. She took a deep breath, lifted her head and looked at Sheik Ali, "As you wish. It is your project."

Sheik Ali nodded, graciously accepting her recognition of his authority. She looked at the women but they avoided eye contact with her.

Nur walked home with Katherine. "Signora Blake, we cannot do a place like that in Hamar Wein. It is too different. We cannot lock it. Many poor people will come and go in and use it and make it dirty and not good."

"I want Sheik Ali to talk with me and tell me why he did not like my idea."

Nur shrugged and said nothing.

Katherine found Dan at the dining room table. He was sorting and stacking newspapers. "The plane from Rome came in today with the mail. I put your magazines on the bed. Look at this. It will take me weeks to read through these. I'm going to arrange the papers by date and read from the earliest to the latest. No peeking ahead." He paused. "What's wrong? You look upset."

"More like fed-up. I had an idea and Sheik Ali simply rejected it. He won't talk with me. Is it because I'm a woman? Is he such an important man that he doesn't have to explain anything? When I think about it maybe he was right. Sheik Ali's women probably don't do the laundry. They have lots of women servants. And they have running water in their house. The place I had in mind would be for other women, the ones who have to haul water to their houses. I didn't think about who would manage the place and take care of it. Anyhow, I'm still mad and I need to calm down."

"Forget it! What makes you think you can change anything here. And what does it get you? You can't really be friends with people so different from you. What you're trying to do is impossible. Think about something else."

"Think about what? Besides the kids, just keeping house and parties? Nothing more than that?"

Planning for the project continued and the development agency wrote a contract for the Sheik to sign. Katherine read and reread it, several times. It lacked a critical clause she feared could lead to a major, if not disastrous, conflict. She asked Nur to arrange a meeting.

"Sheik Ali, the only men's work in the development agency's budget is for making cement and, maybe, laying drain pipes. I talked with the Director and he said they pay for supplies. Not for labor. How will you organize to get the work done?"

As Sheik Ali absorbed the information, he looked surprised and then resolute. "We will pay men to dig and do the dirty work."

"And how much will that cost?"

"I will find out."

After several days Sheik Ali informed Katherine that the cost was higher than the community could possibly afford.

She responded, "You have many unemployed healthy young men in Hamar Wein, especially where you and your friends live, where most of the paving will be done. Why can't they do the work?"

"Because our ancestors held slaves. When I was a child slaves did everything for us. Our young men do not do base, demeaning labor." Nur, feeling his English not adequate for Sheik Ali's meaning, used only Italian.

Katherine said, "Then we may not get the streets paved. The rains begin again in four or five months."

"The agency should do the work for us."

Her anger returned. "I do not agree." She added, muttering, "What in the hell am I doing here?" followed immediately by instructions to Nur, "Don't translate that."

Katherine left abruptly. Nur walked with her to her house. She mused aloud, not expecting a response, "This is it. We're done, through. Anyhow, Sheik Ali doesn't appreciate anything I have done for him or the project. He has never thanked me, not once."

"Signora Blake, it is foreigners who are saying 'Thank you.' You are an American lady, very fine and rich. Is our saying thank you important? You have everything."

"Your mother made an embroidered headscarf for me. Women have made cakes and samosas for me. Those are nice gestures. They mean a lot to me."

"When the project will be finished you will see. We will be happy together."

Katherine said nothing. She was not ready to tell Nur that even if the latest problem were solved and if the paving were done, she would not see it finished. Dan had been transferred. She and the children would be leaving Somalia in two weeks.

The following morning Nur entered the house to find Katherine sitting on the living room floor, wrapping paintings she had taken down from the walls. Fighting back tears, she, at last, told him. He quickly excused himself and, adding further to Katherine's blues, stayed away for a week. Even Sharif could not give her news of Sheik Ali and Nur.

When Nur finally returned he spoke in the same formal manner he had assumed on the day Sheik Ali originally asked her to visit him in his home. "Sheik Ali is asking to see you this morning."

Katherine sighed. She said she could not leave the house before the afternoon. She was packing and had to have their possessions ready by noon for shipping.

Nur walked with Katherine to a four o'clock meeting, guiding her through the maze of Hamar Wein streets by a path not familiar to her. He stopped at a three-story building. They entered and climbed a stairway to the roof.

As the flat roof came into view, Katherine saw Sheik Ali seated on a chair. He was dressed in new clothes, as he had been on the day he called on her in her home. Beside him was the only other chair. It was empty. Sitting around the edges of the roof, on three sides so the Sheik could see them, were men she did not know. A few were gray and bent with age but most, about thirty men, were in their middle years, strong, authoritative looking men. Some twenty younger men and adolescent boys lounged here and there, quietly observing.

Katherine sensed immediately that she had stepped into a meeting of the council of elders. She was being admitted to the inner sanctum, being permitted to watch the governing body of Hamar Wein's dominant clan.

This was Katherine's first time on an empty rooftop. She could hear sea gulls calling and ocean waves breaking on the shore below. The air stirred gently and tasted slightly salt on her lips. The sun was gliding toward the horizon. At approximately six o'clock it would disappear and darkness would descend, without an intervening twilight, as if a lamp had been turned off. The meeting must begin. Sheik Ali gestured for her to sit beside him. Nur stepped behind them and stationed himself between the chairs.

The Sheik spoke, "Katherine, we are saddened by your departure from us. Before you leave, we should resolve all difficulties." To convey the poetry and eloquence of Sheik Ali's language, Nur translated into Italian rather than English.

Sheik Ali turned to the elders and instructed them to decide. Would they permit the young men of Hamar Wein to dig with shovels, haul dirt in wheelbarrows, carry loads and labor like commoners to pave the streets of their city?

An animated discussion began, lead by two men with, it seemed to Katherine, arguments well prepared in advance. She asked Nur for an explanation.

"The old man, the gray beard man sitting over there, he is not liking the project. He is saying we are okay. The old ways are best. But Mohamed, the man sitting over here, is - how do you say? - real sharp and these days the men are hearing him. He is saying 'get those streets paved.' Sheik Ali is saying stop talking, talking, all the time talking, and decide. They must all say one thing."

The sun slipped away. In the near dark the oldest man announced the consensus: their men should do the work. The young men murmured their agreement. Sheik Ali officially informed Katherine.

Katherine, eyes misting with tears, said, "Thank you. Now my leaving will be a little less sad for me."

Sheik Ali responded, "Your people and my people will always be friends."

Six months later Katherine received two letters from Mogadiscio, one from Nancy, her American friend, and the other from the Director. He wrote to let her know that the project had been an outstanding success for their development agency. Both letters included a clipping from the local Italian language newspaper. The newspaper article began with a photograph of Sheik Ali directing several young men to lift their first shovel full of dirt from the street. The men wore specially made caps and shirts. Across the front of the cap and on the pocket of the shirt was a phrase in Somali, embroidered by a mother or wife or sister: "For the Glory of Our City". The men were not common laborers; they were volunteers honorably serving their community.

Sheik Ali was quoted. "I have always dreamed of returning Hamar Wein to its former beauty but the success of this project and its very existence is because of Miss Katherine Blake, who so encouraged us in our endeavors. ... "

Cathedral and Governor's Palace facing one another, Bar Nazionale on the corner to the right of the Cathedral, Croce del Sud with interior courtyard to the left of the Governor's Palace.

Cathedral and residences for nuns and priests.

103

Governor's Palace, later the Prime Minister's Office.

A wing of the Governor's Palace and the Croce del Sud Hotel viewed from the Cathedral tower. Via Roma is behind the Governor's Palace and the hotel.

Triumphal Arch with Govenor's Palace in foreground.

Municipio – City Hall.

Arba Ruqun Mosque minaret seen from the Municipio garden pavilion.

Arch, Minaret, Municipio and Museum on Corso Vittorio Emanuele.

106

National Museum on Corso Vittorio Emanuele, facing the ocean, formerly a Zanzibar era residence.

The Italian fishmarket became a café at the shore.

National Assembly, later used as the Municipio.

Middle School.

Banco di Roma established in 1936.

Credito Somalo established in 1954 as the new government's bank.

Downtown street with the 1950s Banco di Roma to the left and a building of shops, arcade and second story apartments.

Store with second story residence.

The first of many cinemas in Mogadiscio.

Corso Vittorio Emanuele to the ocean—Zanzibar Customs House above rooftops on left, Post Office at the far street corner, Hamar Wein behind buildings on the right.

The old harbor and Zanzibar Customs House. The two large apartment buildings are Italian. In the center are Italian buildings on Corso Vittorio Emanuele.

Harbor and Zanzibar Customs House in the 1950s.

MOGADISCIO

NEL MAPPAMONDO DI FRA MAURO, CARTOGRAFO DELLA REPUBBLICA DI VENEZIA (1460)

Edizione a cura del Comune di Venezia. (*Riproduzione gentilmente autorizzata*)

Mogadiscio by Fra Mauro 1460.

113

Left: Sofala 1683. From November to March the monsoon winds come onto the coast at Mogadiscio and cut out at Sofala in Mozambique. From April to October they reverse.

Below: Drawings by Fra Mauro of ships that sailed to city-states along the East Africa coast.

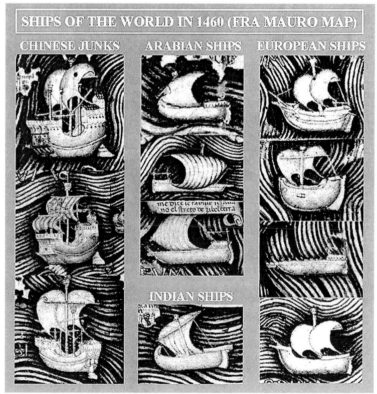

SHIPS OF THE WORLD IN 1460 (FRA MAURO MAP)

CHINESE JUNKS   ARABIAN SHIPS   EUROPEAN SHIPS

INDIAN SHIPS

View of Mogadiscio in 1847. Most of the buildings from this point to the Jama Mosque minaret in the background were leveled to build the Italian Mogadiscio.

Mogadiscio 1882.

Jama Mosque 1950s.

Jama Mosque Inscription above the minaret door 1950s.

Engraving of Fakr Ud-Din mosque built in 1269 C.E. in Mogadiscio.

Houses in Hamar Wein along the Lungo Mare, the ocean road.

Hamar Wein apartment building on the ocean road in about 1905. The man with the fez may be a policeman. In the background on the left are women in the veil.

Wattle-daub houses in the fishermen's compound at the ocean shore.

Weavers in Hamar Wein. They sit under a canopy working horizontal looms.

Weaver 1882.

Women spinning cotton 1882.

People of Hamar Wein in 1938.

A roadside tea stand on the Strada Imperiale outside Mogadiscio.

Women near the river behind Mogadiscio loading wooden containers of camels' milk to sell in the markets of Mogadiscio.

Somalis trying to sell a bizarre wood carving to my husband. Azad is watching.

Woman with the family's pack camel, ready for moving to a new camp site.

LEARNING TO DANCE

Hussein had changed. I do not mean to imply that previously he had been frivolous or ill behaved. He had been somewhat less conventional and certainly more open than other young men in his community, but still, he had never done anything untoward or disquieting. He had shown great respect for his elders. He never smoked in front of them. He listened attentively to their teachings in the mosque. He obeyed his father, and like a good son, he abstained from wine and womanizing. All this was admirable but now I wondered. I thought he had gone too far. His new conformity to the community's every tenet seemed excessive and so encompassing that it stole away his spirit, even robbed him of his good looks. That, at least, was how I perceived him when, at last, he came to visit us. He had changed and I felt sad for him.

It was 1966; Raj and I and our children were again in Mogadiscio. I was happy to return and looked forward to seeing friends, especially Hussein and the others from Mogadiscio's small Indian community of shopkeepers. During our previous stay, in 1963-64, they had been wonderfully helpful to us. As traditionally Muslim as they were, they still recognized Raj as one of their own. They had known immediately from his name that he was of Hindu background and therefore somewhat different from them, but he was Indian nevertheless and spoke two of their languages, Hindustani and English. They were surprised at his having an American wife but they accepted me.

We were fortunate. Without them, setting up our home and adjusting to Mogadiscio's simple, low technology mode of daily life could have been far more difficult than it turned out to be. Somalia was like stepping back in time, to a land of scarcity and strange customs, but the Indians knew what we needed to live safely and comfortably. They guided us in renting a house, purchasing furniture, equipping the kitchen, shopping for food.

Hussein was especially helpful and knowledgeable. He was one of the few Indian men who had ventured after Somalia's independence into the Italian colonial center of Mogadiscio for employment, to mix with Italians, to find his way among those who controlled the truly profitable businesses, the enterprises importing European goods to be sold at a handsome profit to foreigners. He became an accountant and general cultural go-between for a firm that dealt with several Embassies and various United Nations development programs.

He had everything he needed for success; he was personable, experienced in business, fluent in English and Italian. He dressed, as was appropriate for a young man of substance, in dark trousers, an open-necked white shirt, shoes and stockings rather than sandals. He appeared always in a hurry but agreeable, asking questions, giving information. His knowledge about Mogadiscio was total; he knew everyone, knew where to buy anything, knew the value of most items available on the market and how much to pay for each.

I became increasingly involved with the Indian community. The fact that they lived, had their shops and their mosque in the casbah was a definite plus for me. The casbah, Hamar Wein, intrigued me, and because Indian men were there in shops I could visit, Raj felt comfortable with my roaming its byways, exploring and learning about their world. The Indian men talked with me and they took me to their homes to meet the women and children. When I agreed to teach in the Indian school at the mosque I came to know the boys and challenged them to learn about the world outside Hamar Wein.

A number of Indian men regularly visited Raj and me at home. Often, in the late afternoon, after siesta, when they were rounding, on their rounds of visits, *circolare* in Italian, they stopped by to talk and have tea with us. Hussein was the youngest and the liveliest and the one most engaged in all the discussions. He freely expressed his opinions, in detail and at length, on any topic, as if to invite disagreement. At times he and I did disagree and we would argue. The other men were more typical in their style of conversation; they were circumspect, more cautious and guarded.

One argument I thought I had lost irretrievably. I was aware of the Indian men's traditional thinking but had underestimated just how thoroughly traditional it was. They firmly believed that the sun and stars and the planets, which they could name, revolved around the earth. My attempts to persuade them otherwise were useless. I had only my faith in astronomy to counter their arguments. I could sketch a rough picture of the earth and other planets circling the sun, but I could think of no indisputable evidence to persuade them that my view of reality was the true one.

In an earlier argument about the nature of our earth, my view had prevailed. This was a discussion about whether the earth is round or flat. In an Arabic book that their religious leader, the Sayyid, had read to them the earth was described as flat but the men had never heard of anyone falling off. They traveled frequently to Aden, the British port in Yemen, to purchase goods they sold wholesale or in their shops, and they occasionally flew to Nairobi or Karachi. They knew that Somalis went to Italy and foreigners from everywhere were coming to Mogadiscio. The earth seemed to have no end. As we sat in conversation over tea and biscuits, I told them I recalled reading that when one looks out over the ocean and watches a ship approaching from the horizon, the top of the ship comes first into view and then the lower parts, as if the ship were rising toward you. If the earth were flat the entire ship would be visible from the first sighting. They took note and said they would observe for themselves how a ship appears as it approaches from the horizon. They later confirmed that what I had said was true. Clear reasoning and empirical evidence convinced them, after all, that the earth is round.

For our argument about the sun and stars and planets, I had no such proof, and the Indian men had all the information they thought they needed. Everyone they knew pictured a stationary earth with the sun and moon and stars in motion around it. When they told the Sayyid in the mosque about our discussion he read them eloquent poetic verses from the Koran about the earth and the sun and moon and stars and seven heavens in harmony. I had no knowledge that could counter poetry with science.

I tried for weeks to think of a proof and had given up when one morning Hussein came to the house and sat quietly with me under the bougainvillea arbor.

He said, "I have been thinking. John Glenn went into outer space in a rocket. Very high. Is that true?

"Yes, of course it's true. In the Friendship 7. He even circled the earth."

Hussein shook his head as if to resettle out-of-place pieces back into their proper slots. "Did he go straight up into the sky? Didn't he crash into anything?"

So that was it! At last I understood Hussein's model of the universe. A phrase from long ago school days floated into my mind: "the music of the spheres." Hussein's community's cosmology was based on the second century Ptolemaic system. The verse from the Koran, "seven heavens in harmony," seemed consistent with this view. The system visualized the sun and moon and planets being moved by spheres that rotate around the earth and, in Hussein's thinking, those spheres had to be substantial physical things to support such weight. Like everyone else, Hussein had read in April 1961 about Yuri Gagarin rocketing into space, but he dismissed the event as unimportant. After all, the Russians were communists and did not believe in business. Besides, who could trust a nation of atheists? Americans, as his fellow Indians confirmed, were a god-fearing people who appreciated businessmen and dealt fairly with them. When Americans launched a rocket that went straight up, unimpeded, far, far above the earth one had to pay attention. This was believable evidence that the sky held no spheres. Hussein would reconsider his cosmology. The American woman might be right after all.

Hussein was twenty-five in 1963. At that time he had been married for eight years. In 1955, his father sailed to Zanzibar, following through on correspondence with an unusually traditional family from its Indian Shia community, to arrange a marriage between one of their daughters and Hussein's older brother, who had reached his eighteenth birthday. The father was well received by the family. He found them respectable and a good family with whom to establish a kinship alliance. They kept their women in strict purdah and relative leisure, always indoors, out of the sun, because the men could afford servants for outside work. One proof of the family's wealth was their women's etiolated skin, considered a mark of feminine beauty. (It made me think of the pale asparagus favored in French haute cuisine.) The women were also, as the men assured prospective fathers-in-law, fertile and likely to produce many sons. Hussein's father approved of the girl intended for his older son and decided, as long as he was arranging one marriage, to arrange a second; it would cost him only a little additional trouble. He asked to take along a younger sister for Hussein. The double wedding would be less expensive and keeping sisters together generally resulted in a less disputatious household.

Forget that neither the boys nor the girls had time to be young, to give rein to the imagination, to discover alternative selves before assuming the responsibilities of adulthood. A boy became a man at puberty and a girl a woman at first menstruation.

I visited Hussein's family in their home. He and his wife and children and two brothers and their wives and children lived with the mother and father and an unmarried sister in a two-story house. With Hussein as interpreter, I spent time with the women and small children. From what I observed, the older brother and his wife had an affectionate relationship, but Hussein and his wife seemed like strangers with one

127

another. I occasionally heard old men in the community speak sentimentally and appreciatively of their wives, but nevertheless, given the chasm between the men's daily life and the women's, matching personalities was seldom a major consideration when parents were arranging marriages for their children. A bride coming into a joint household spent far more time with her mother-in-law than with her husband. She had to work for and with her mother-in-law hour after hour, day after day, along with her sisters-in-law, in the labor-intensive activities of running a household.

A husband and wife were seldom alone together, except in bed. It is reasonable to assume that when Hussein's father chose the bridal sisters for his family his intention was to please his wife and ensure peace of mind for himself. If, incidentally, he brought happiness to the young couple, all the better. He probably thought that the husband and wife would in time become fond of, perhaps in love with, one another. In many marriages this happened. For others, it did not and left an emotional emptiness that could never be filled.

Hussein was a good father. He often had a child or two with him when he came visiting. On Id al Fitr, the day ending Ramadan, the lunar month of fasting, he brought all three to the house for us to admire and to offer sweets and candies. They looked scrubbed and self-conscious in their new clothes. The boys were dressed as miniatures of their father, and the girl wore a frock of bright shiny fabric and ribbons in her hair. I thought of how, decades before, I was given my new dress for the year on Easter Sunday, the day that ends Lent, the Christian period of fasting.

As a thoughtful friend, Hussein could not have been surpassed. He had learned that I, unlike my dear husband, was inordinately fond of movies, so he showed me the one cinema in town, on Via Roma near Hamar Wein, where I might see what he considered good films. It was an open-air theater in a large courtyard, with chairs set in rows and a white wall serving as the screen, originally owned by an Italian then sold to a Somali. Mogadiscio Indians, with their puritanical strictures against much of what might be shown on the screen, would not invest in such a business. This cinema was, of course, like most of the cinemas in town, intended for men only, but custom did accept that an occasional family man would bring his mother or wife with him to see a movie. Hussein took me as his guest and we saw "Awara," the most popular Indian film of the year. It is a good film and still holds up today as worth seeing. Raj Kapoor played the lead. He sang and danced. His son, Shashi Kapoor, a boy then and later an internationally known actor, played the Raj character as a child. The love interest and heroine was pictured as a professional woman, a lawyer. As we watched the movie Hussein translated the Hindi into English and gave me a running commentary on the plot and characters. Walking back to our house, I congratulated him on his skills as interpreter, but he demurred. This had been his eleventh time seeing "Awara," and he knew the movie by heart.

Films from India were the favorites throughout Africa and Asia in those years. The most popular featured singing and elaborately choreographed dancing that invariably occupied half the film footage. The hero was brave and handsome. The heroine was ravishingly beautiful, impossibly virtuous. There was no nudity, kissing or overtly sexual behavior. The actresses dressed modestly, as befits the mores of audiences in traditional cultures, but a trick was devised for revealing the heroine's physical charms: at some point the plot required her to walk into a pool of water or stand in the rain. and voila, we had the wet sari scene. Story lines were simple, often improbable, but they told of romance and the triumph of good over evil, all staged in beautiful settings. From my experience, adult men were as vulnerable as any teenage girl to the dream world on the screen.

A Somali man told me that when an Indian movie arrived in Mogadiscio, among the first persons in the long queue buying tickets for its opening night were the tailors from Hamar

Wein. By morning they had stitched up dresses adapted from the film and hung them in front of their shops. For weeks after a new movie opened, Somali men stopped Indian boys on the street, sang in flawless Hindi to them snatches of the film's songs and asked for a translation. When Raj first went to Turkey and Russia in the 1960s, before most people in those countries had ever seen anyone from India, strangers greeted him with tunes from "Awara."

The King and I, one of my favorite films, came to town, to the Cinema Nazionale, the only theatre in Mogadiscio that was under a roof, had electric lighting and cushioned seats arranged in rows on a floor that sloped upwards from the screen. It even had a balcony equally well furnished and comfortable. It and a cinema near the Cathedral were the two patronized by foreigners and the more urbanized, affluent Somalis. They were cinemas that a woman could acceptably attend alone. Given a modern cinema nearby and Raj away for a few days and our trusted guard, Ahmed, in the house, I tucked the children into bed and went off alone to see "The King and I." When the film ended I skipped home, possessed by its movement and music, to find Hussein sitting under the bougainvillea arbor. I wanted to dance, just like Anna, in a gorgeous swirling gown and could not bring myself to sit down. Hussein confessed to me, in a shy voice not typical for him, that he had never danced but was fascinated by this sinful pastime of a boy and girl close together, in full public view, moving as one to a melody.

I had watched Indian boys sitting rigidly upright on straight-backed chairs, listening to a popular tune on the phonograph, tightly restraining themselves from the slightest twitch of response. On impulse, I boldly took this boy by the hand, pulled him up from his chair, told him to watch my feet and step as I did. Then, singing loudly but probably not in tune, I waltzed him around the compound as he gracefully fell into the rhythm. Shall we DANCE?; one, two, three; Shall we DANCE? Shall we dance? Shall we dance? We circled round and around and around. Ahmed and his buddies who kept him company at night in our compound stopped mid-phrase in their interminable stream of small talk and stared at us, open-mouthed and amazed. Hussein and I took one last turn, dizzily plunked ourselves down in the chairs and sat there laughing, gratefully accepting the glasses of orange soda Ahmed had ready for us.

Soon after our "dance," Raj's sabbatical in Somalia had come to an end, and we returned home. Now, two and a half years later, again in Mogadiscio, I asked people about Hussein. He had not visited us, and yet, he must have heard we were in town.

This time I knew the city. We enrolled our children in the American school, located a good house to rent, bought furniture and supplies, hired Ahmed and Asha from our previous stay in Mogadiscio to help me make a home for us. Raj began his work. Several weeks passed. At last, Hussein came to call, as always, unannounced.

Ahmed opened the compound gate, and I watched Hussein from the verandah as he walked up the driveway. For a moment, I did not recognize him. If we had met on the street I might have passed him by as if he were a stranger. He had not changed weight, lost his hair, put on eyeglasses or been disfigured in any way, but he looked to be a different person. His once slightly hunch-shouldered, relaxed posture had become hunched-over, hollow-chested and graceless. His expression was pinched and harsh. In just two years, the looseness and freedom of youth had left him.

I said, "What a pleasure to see you. Please come in and have tea with me."

"No, I am in a hurry. I was passing by. I bring you greetings from my father and mother. I will sit here for a minute."

He sat down on a verandah chair, stiff and upright, a leather briefcase balanced on his knees. I slipped away to the kitchen, returned with two cups of tea and sat opposite him. He did not put out his hand for the tea, so I placed his cup on the table between us. He did not touch it. I asked him about his health and the health of his family. He said that all were fine, and I accepted that as the truth. If anything unfortunate or drastic had happened to Hussein while we were away I would have heard about it from the two young men from the community, distant cousins of Hussein, who occasionally came to visit us. They had been to America and wanted to keep contact with Americans.

Hussein set his briefcase on the floor, picked it up, fidgeted with it. "I hear you are spending time with Sheik Ali and his lineage. You go around with the Somalis and visit them in their houses."

"Yes. The Sheik and I are working together on a project to pave the streets of Hamar Wein. The Somalis came and asked me to help."

"You did not come to us, the Indians, to talk about this."

"I tried to find you. Where have you been? You aren't working with the Italian firm. I looked for you there. I wanted to visit your family, but the men are out of the house all day, and I haven't anyone to translate for me with the women. Besides, I have been very busy. Living in Mogadiscio as a foreigner isn't all that easy. You probably know that Raj is consulting with the government this time. He doesn't have much free time. I have to keep a big house and do a lot of entertaining with the Embassies and Somali officials. Why don't the Indians come anymore for afternoon tea?

"My father and uncles came once to your house."

"Oh, my. That's true. I'm sorry."

The Indians had, indeed, stopped by. I invited them into the house, to the living room, where three Somali guests, carrying on in Italian, were joking and telling Raj mildly ribald, funny stories about their experiences in Rome. They were already on their third glass of chilled grapefruit juice well spiked with gin. The Indian men did not sit down. The use of alcohol was forbidden in their community. The Somali men's behavior was offensive to them. They excused themselves, said they were expected at home, and allowed me to see them to the gate. That was the last I saw of them.

For a moment I considered expressing my regrets to Hussein. Instead, I said, "Where are you working now?"

"I quit the Italians."

I thought I caught a note of disappointment in his voice. "But why? You were doing so well with them. And they paid you well."

Ever so slightly, Hussein shrugged. "I liked the job but my father did not approve of me mixing so much with foreigners. He said it interfered with my going to the mosque. The elders were criticizing him for it."

He added, a little defiantly, "You are only half right about how the Italians paid me. It was all right, considering I am Indian, but they paid their Italian accountant twice as much and he was very lazy. I did not say that to the boss, I just told him my uncles needed me for the wholesale side of our family businesses."

"Do you enjoy working for the family?

"Yes. It is my family. I travel often, mostly to Aden to import goods from China and India. Next year I will go on the Haj to Mecca."

"I hear you have your oldest child in the American school and he is a bright boy."

"My family is growing. I have had another son since you left."

We exchanged a few pleasantries. He stood up and said a formal farewell. I asked him to give my regards to his wife and parents. I escorted him to the gate and watched as he walked away. Two years ago he would have been almost running. Now he walked carefully, deliberately, like any other man in his community.

Raj and I spent a busy, productive year in Mogadiscio, he with government officials and the diplomatic set and I on a project with Somalis in Hamar Wein. Our paths no longer regularly crossed those of Hussein, and when we did meet conversation was minimal. Finally, all too soon for me, the time came for our family to return home. I went looking for Hussein to bid him good-bye, but he was away on a business trip.

We left in 1967. In 1969, a military dictator seized power in a coup d'etat and established a "scientific socialist" state in Somalia. He dissolved the National Assembly, assassinated or imprisoned political leaders, banned civil organizations, took control of the media and forbade all dissent. He turned to the Soviet Union for economic, technical and military assistance. Many educated Somalis left the country.

I wondered how the Indian community would react to the oppression and impending economic disaster. How would they protect themselves from the inevitable cataclysm?

Certainly, they could not react as they had previously. In January 1948, when Mogadiscio was under the British and Hussein was old enough to remember the events, Somalis in Mogadiscio had gone on a rampage against the Italians and, almost incidentally, against the Indians. For days men ran through the streets, looting and killing. Not all Somalis were culpable; friendly Somalis in Hamar Wein protected vulnerable Indian families. However, most Indians were prepared. They had expected the periodic pogrom and constructed their houses in such a way that they could barricade themselves inside and wait out the emotional storm. When peace returned, they made themselves socially invisible. Indian women, carefully veiled, seldom walked outside their immediate neighborhood. The men avoided conflict, behaved unobtrusively, dressed modestly, never flaunted their wealth. They organized ever more tightly around their mosque, their shops and their houses, huddling together in their ghetto, closing in on themselves and their traditions.

Would they think this survival strategy could still suffice? Through the years, as the situation in Somalia deteriorated, I watched from afar. Men from Mogadiscio kept Raj informed. The news was not good; the Indians seemed unprepared for their inevitable flight from disaster. Many of the families would not have survived if the community from Mombasa had not sent a ship to Mogadiscio in 1991, only a few days before total anarchy, to rescue the Shia Indians.

But several years before that dramatic event we were hearing odd things about Hussein from our contacts in Mogadiscio. He had taken to contradicting the elders in the mosque and once, in full public view, he had disagreed with his father. Such disgraceful behavior! I inferred from the gist of the stories that Hussein saw sooner than others Somalia's imminent implosion. He was trying to convince them that the departure of Americans and Western Europeans from Mogadiscio portended deep trouble, worse than ever before. He reminded them about Uganda's expulsion of all Indians, warning them that it could happen to their own community. He wanted the community to move, to seek a better future elsewhere, but he seemed not to be heard.

As the situation deteriorated and he watched other young men move their families outside Somalia, Hussein acted. Possibly he travelled on a Pakistani passport; the Somali government continued to deny a passport, the sign of citizenship, to Indians. Somehow, though, he maneuvered or bribed his way around this major inconvenience and acquired official papers of some sort. However inspired and however he managed, several years before Mogadiscio metamorphosed into an inferno he picked up his wife and children and escaped to Rome. He took with him a hoard of gold jewelry and tapped into an Italian bank account to finance their first few months in exile.

Soon after arriving in Rome, he contacted men he had known in the Italian firms at home and they advised him on where and how to open a store. He began with a small enterprise, selling imported goods from India and China, as his father and uncles were doing in Mogadiscio, and gradually expanded the store. In Italy he became a proper and respected businessman who need not hide his prosperity.

His wife, after a few months of feeling out of place on the streets among Italian women, threw away her dark, enveloping purdah robes. I imagine her emerging from them as from a chrysalis.

Tucked into the long, dutiful letters Hussein wrote home were references to his many Italian friends. He did not directly say he preferred his new life to life in his own community, but men in Mogadiscio could read between the lines, and they were dismayed. Elders in the mosque protested to everyone who would listen that Hussein was losing his religion and that he was being seduced into utter decadence by Italy's wicked, enthralling atmosphere.

I wonder if he ever learned to dance.

CAPITALISM MOGADISCIO STYLE

The man looked out of place. I felt quite certain he was Somali, and his presence in Southall surprised me. In the spring of 1992 refugees from Somalia were still something of a novelty. As he walked toward me, I grew ever more curious. I was tempted to approach him, American style in this British setting, and ask him what in the world he was doing among all these Indians in London's little India.

Of course, he could have asked the same about me. My reason for being there was my husband, Raj. We were visiting his cousin, Kamla, on our way back to the States from Paris, and at that moment, he and she were totally engrossed in shopping, selecting things the three of us had driven miles and miles to buy, special treats such as oily hot pickles and savory snacks available only in a well stocked Indian grocery store. I had opted out, bored with following them around as they slowly examined nearly everything they saw, checking on brand names and reading labels, reminiscing about scents and flavors from their childhood years in Bombay, moving about as if in a trance.

At last I implored Raj, "Honey, would you mind if I went to the car? You really don't need me here."

"Sorry. The nostalgia gets to me. Kamla and I can hurry this along."

"No, don't hurry. If you give me the key, I'll take the stuff you've already decided on and put it in the trunk. Then you two can take your time."

Kamla gave me her most engaging smile. "Oh dear! We haven't gone to the *mitai walla* yet. There's sure to be a long queue there, but they make the best Indian sweets in England and I want you and Raj to taste them. You go ahead. Walk about and enjoy yourself."

Raj handed me a basket of jars, packets, boxes and cans. "You won't mind checking these out and taking them with you?"

"Not at all. See you at the car in half an hour, or whenever you're ready."

I made my way to the counter and leaned across to look more closely at a Hindu shrine poised on the shelf behind it, at small oil lamps and diminutive god figures sculpted in brass. The storeowner checked each of our purchases and noted their prices on a scrap of paper, to be entered into the cash register when Raj and Kamla would be finished with replenishing her Indian pantry. I filled the three string bags we had brought with us. The owner opened the door for me, and dangling our treasures from both hands, I left the store's encompassing aroma of spices for the cool air of springtime.

The streets were crowded and bright with the colors of India. Hindu women were in sari, with a red *tika* in the center of the forehead. I caught bits of conversation among others in *camise-silvar*, a long blouse over pajama, and heard Muslim names. The hijab had not yet become widely adopted. I saw no woman in the veil. Most of the men wore a properly dark conservative suit, and a few had mustache and beard and sported the handsomely wrapped Sikh turban. Teenagers dressed no differently than other teenagers in Britain. Grandmotherly women looked after babies and small children while the middle generation busied themselves in the food shops and browsed the clothing stores for Indian sandals, gold jewelry and the latest fashions from home.

Kamla had parked her dark blue Vauxhall on a residential street, a pleasant five-minute walk away. On reaching the car, I opened its trunk, or *boot*, as she would have said, placed our things inside, closed the trunk, then paused to survey the scene and plan the stroll I intended to take. The houses were arranged differently from those in the neighborhoods I had known in my own Midwestern American towns.

They were row on neat row of narrow detached brick structures, each with a well-composed little garden of bushes and flowers in front and a brick walkway from the small porch to the sidewalk.

People walked by me. Except for this one man, they were all Indian and in a post-shopping mode, carrying packages, resolutely on their way somewhere, probably home. The non-Indian man was neatly dressed, about fifty years old, tall, a bit heavyset, dark skin, fine-featured, with black wavy hair. He walked slowly, as if uncertain where to turn next.

When he stopped to look around, as I had seen him do several times, I approached him and said, "You are Somali, aren't you?"

"Yes, I am."

"And you look as if you are from the north."

"That is right." He smiled, obviously proud of his identity and pleased to have it recognized.

"I heard on BBC this morning that the Marehan are practically at war with the Issaq. The Marehan are Siyaad Barre's clan, aren't they? I heard that northerners in Mogadiscio were being dragged from their homes, even executed."

"I am Issaq. Yes, it is true."

"What is going on? The violence sounds horrible. What is happening in Mogadiscio? I lived there for two years and loved the city. Tell me what is happening."

"Somalia is falling apart. The inflation is terrible. Sometimes in one month pasta doubles in price. It keeps getting worse. Sugar is too expensive to buy, even for me. I got out."

"And your family?"

"My sons went to Riyadh to work but my wife wanted to come here. We went to Delhi and stayed there for a year. Friends helped get us visas for Britain."

"Will you go back to Somalia?"

"I do not think so. Right now we are staying with a nephew in Tower Hamlets but I am looking around. I need to find a job. Everything I own is in Mogadiscio. My Mercedes Benz, two televisions and all the furniture I brought back from Aden. I saw street boys starting to loot my house as soon as we got into the airport taxi. One of them was ripping out the copper wiring. They will probably sell all my things for guns. I suppose the government has taken over my other houses. I had five. Used to get good rent from the foreigners."

Suddenly, I realized why this man looked so familiar to me. I blurted out, "You are Omar Hussein."

He looked puzzled. "Have we met before?"

Yes. We had met before. We met in September 1966, on the second day of the second time I lived in Somalia, at a moment when I was feeling happy to be in Mogadiscio, the capital city, and delighted with the prospect of moving with my family into an especially nice house next door to an agreeable family.

In 1966, Raj and I knew Mogadiscio well. We had been away only two years and had kept in touch with people and events in the city. We anticipated no difficulties with settling in. Houses to rent were easily available, ready for the multitude of foreigners arriving to staff the many Embassies, United Nations agencies and development programs. It had not occurred to us that finding a place to live would pose any problem whatsoever.

Our plan was to stay for a few days in a hotel while we enrolled our children in school and looked for a house. Through letters sent months ahead, followed by telegrams, we had reserved rooms in the original Italian colonial hotel, the Croce del Sud, the Southern Cross, and found them ready for us, as promised. Most foreigners considered the Croce a bit too seedy, but I found it charming. I liked the way the whitewashed building opened to a courtyard, with guest rooms off the white-pillared corridors that overlooked the interior garden, the air cooled by its greenery. Italians and Somalis spent hours in the garden patio dining area over a leisurely meal or drinks, meeting friends, relaxing, reading European newspapers bought at the hotel's magazine stand.

Early the first morning we were ready to begin our adventure of another year in Somalia. We walked out of the hotel, into the tropical sun, on to one of Mogadiscio's tree-lined main streets and chanced to meet Anil and Sita, a couple with whom we had been friendly before. We stopped to chat and they welcomed us back.

Sita was holding a two-month-old baby. I said, "She's so cute. May I hold her a minute?" Sita gently transferred the infant to my arms and I knelt so my daughter could hold her tiny hand.

I said, "I thought you would have returned to India by now."

Anil said, "We'll be staying for another two years. You've probably heard the American school's accepting U.N. children now. Didn't you have yours there? Is it a good school?"

My son muttered, "Yeah, we went there. It's not bad." And I added, "It's an excellent school. We've already written and enrolled the kids."

Sita smiled. "That's wonderful to hear. Anil wants to stay on the job but ..."

He interrupted. "I have to finish my assignment. It's for the Horn of Africa locust control project."

"... but the twins are six now. If they don't go to the American school it will be either boarding school in India or me taking them home and leaving Anil here all alone."

Raj said, "Don't worry. The boys will do fine in the school. By the way, we are looking for a house. Know of any available?"

"I know exactly the house for you! And for us, too. Sita has been after me to get a bigger place now that we have the baby. There's a compound near here with two houses in it. Both are empty. Come on, let's you and me go over there right away and see what they look like inside. I know where the owner lives, so we can get the keys."

Anil turned to me. "Would you like to go with Sita and take the children to our house? It's awfully hot out here for them. She will fix lunch for us and we can spend the afternoon together."

Sita and I and the children walked to her home. She nursed the baby and it slept while she and I cooked and the children played on the shady verandah. The husbands soon returned. They had seen the houses, found them highly satisfactory and had discussed terms with the owner, Omar Hussein. He would stop by after lunch with the contract.

From Raj's descriptions of the houses, I thought either would be fine for us. They were large and seemed well designed. We would have three bedrooms and a good bathroom. From what Raj said, the kitchen must have been almost modern. The living room opened onto a terrace, which would be perfect for the parties I looked forward to giving.

Omar Hussein arrived at the house that afternoon just as I was about to step out from the kitchen. I paused. Anil had told us the landlord spoke English, so I had expected the usual sophisticated Somali who dealt with foreigners, some-one suave, self-confident, dressed in the international style of trousers, shirt and shoes. Omar Hussein was certainly Somali in the self-confident way he carried himself but the clothes he wore, a hosgunti (sarong), white shirt, white rimless cap and rubber flip-flop sandals, were those of an ordinary man.

Anil had already introduced Sita. When I entered the living room and Raj introduced me I sensed that Omar Hussein was as surprised when he saw me as I had been on seeing him, but he quickly turned to discussing the business at hand. He said that after talking with Anil and Raj another couple had offered him a much higher rent for the houses, but if we were willing to match that amount he would be pleased to rent to us.

Raj said, "We are here on a research grant and can't afford to pay that much."

Anil asked, "Isn't that high for those houses, especially in that location? That's almost the rate for the big houses where the top officials live, out at the beach, near the Lido.

"And you're asking more than Indians can pay. We thought about moving into the U. N. family compound. It has a tennis court and a place to show movies. Or up the hill, above the National Assembly, in Bondere. Even some of the Americans are paying less than what you are asking. They have a new apartment building. It's near their school on Kilometer 4. We know an American secretary who's moving in there."

Omar Hussein listened politely but said no more. Sita waited until he left and speculated that he probably did not have another, higher offer, but had given Anil and Raj the Indian rate and raised it when he saw me, an American. I protested that even the Indian rate was higher than any Somali would have to pay and Anil said that the Somali landlords build to rent to foreigners, not to Somalis.

The following day a Somali friend put us in contact with a man from his lineage who had a house on the market. It was a reasonably good house and compound, one in which we could live comfortably. After much haggling, the friend persuaded this landlord to accept what we considered a fair rent, a bit higher than the Indian rate but lower than the American.

The two houses remained unoccupied for another month. Each time I walked by the compound gate my annoyance with Omar Hussein returned. I never discovered the nationality of the renters but they were not American or I would have known. I doubt that whoever it was paid the American rate.

Why was Omar Hussein behaving so irrationally? His actions toward us, his property and the money involved made no sense to me. He was far from being a stupid man. Why was his reasoning about money and investment so different from mine? I needed to understand. Were he and I living in the same economy?

I talked with Somali friends about Omar Hussein and they asked around for me. I learned he had grown up in the north when it was British Somaliland and had learned English while attending, for three years, a British elementary school for boys. Otherwise, he had spent his childhood and youth as a typical pastoral nomad, in continual movement across a semi-arid landscape in search of feed and water for the family's camels, sheep and goats. In 1960, with his wife and small child, he headed south for Mogadiscio, walking and catching an occasional ride in the jeep of an official on tour of duty in the countryside. Once in the city he located the wattle and daub neighborhood where his lineage resided and moved his family in with a cousin.

Then he looked to earning a living. Another cousin, one well placed in the Ministry of Education, found him a job with a United Nations project. He rose quickly from office worker to interpreter for the foreign staff. When we met him he was still new to being an entrepreneur.

Omar Hussein was blessed with good luck. He had arrived in Mogadiscio soon after Somalia's independence, at a time when the Italian colonial city had opened to Somalis as a place to live and work and when a new type of economy had materialized. Foreigners in the tens of thousands descended on Somalia's new capital. They opened embassies. They lived a modern sector lifestyle on international level incomes, had import privileges and shopped in the Italian stores using British pounds, Italian lira and dollars. Sleek black limousines and Land Rovers began to compete with donkey carts, three-wheeled auto rickshaws and Fiat 1100 taxis for space on city streets.

Foreign aid became a major industry. United Nations agencies and many countries, including the United States, initiated development projects. The Common Market contributed an enormous new hospital, prominent and dramatic looking. It remained bare of equipment, and barely used. In those years, the few physicians in Somalia were non-Somali and none of the women giving nursing care were trained nurses. The Chinese, using their own Chinese workers, built a large theater for stage performances. The Somalis used it to practice traditional songs and poetry recitations. The Soviets constructed an over-capacity automated printing press that stood empty while a small, hand-operated Italian press continued churning out government documents. The Somali government could not afford even light bulbs for the new building.

I should add that not all development projects were wrongfully conceptualized and/or badly executed. Several of the United Nation's veterinary programs for sheep and camels were useful. An urban water distributions system was installed. Americans helped establish and staff a teachers' training college that functioned well.

Mogadiscio had entered a boom period. Somalia was receiving more foreign aid per capita than any other African country. As government expanded, a Somali with the proper connections could secure one of the many positions in the many new Ministries, positions that proliferated but might require little more of the occupant than occasionally presenting himself at the office to collect his salary.

All sorts of jobs were created and Somalis willingly left herding camels and planting crops for the easier urban life.

Most of the foreign diplomats, bureaucrats, professionals, technicians and support personnel came with a family. They needed offices, warehouses, workshops, residences and recreation facilities. Labor was needed to erect buildings and lay roads on scrubland where, until independence, only a desultory goat or two had wandered. To live comfortably in a house set in a walled garden and to enjoy a clubhouse at the beach with their compatriots, foreigners hired Somalis and taught them the art of serving an elite. For the numerous vehicles they had shipped in, they trained local men as drivers and mechanics. Clerical positions were available to anyone who spoke and wrote English or Italian.

The economy was still quite simple. Money flowed in but, as yet, there was little in the market to buy. Ordinary Somalis, people working as unskilled or semi-skilled laborers, built houses for themselves, mostly wattle and daub, increasing the size and complexity of Somali *quartiers* that surrounded the Italian Mogadiscio. Men who earned a better income rented or built cinder block houses on previously open land, men such as Omar Hussein when we first met him, traditional traders in livestock or the owner of a restaurant or a cinema. The new Somali elite was evolving: senators in the National Assembly and high-level government officials, plus successful entrepreneurs who contracted with foreigners to build for them or provide them with workers. The elite could afford a modern house and a modern lifestyle, including sending their children to school in Mogadiscio or even in London or Rome.

Most Somalis bought their food and other basic goods from vendors in small markets near their homes. I did not know these markets. Asha, the woman who worked for me, who helped me keep house and care for my family, bought each day's meat and vegetables in the early morning on her way to the house. I bought canned and dry goods in an Arab shop on Via Roma, the street bordering the casbah, Hamar Wein, and staples from back home in the downtown Italian delicatessens and bakeries. Mogadiscio fish was always delicious but I had not grown up eating or cooking fish; I failed to learn about the varieties available and about the fish market in Hamar Wein on the Lungo Mare, the road along the ocean. One could look down from the road to a narrow strip of land at the shore and see into the fishermen's walled compound with its skillfully built, neatly arranged wattle-daub houses, but I never once talked with a fisherman or anyone from the community.

Somalis went into Hamar Wein to buy cloth and household items in the small Indian and Arab shops. Tailors in Hamar Wein cut and stitched clothing and carpenters crafted furniture. I bought my Indian spices in Hamar Wein, but for kitchen and household items and implements I shopped in the glass-fronted Indian stores on Via Roma. Goods from the countryside were for sale in a marketplace outside Hamar Wein: wooden combs and containers, baskets, ropes, mats, knives and tools, as were vegetables grown in an Indian commercial farm and trucked in, plus fruits and other foods produced by village farmers and brought into town in wheelbarrows or on donkey carts. A Hadhramauti Arab had a small factory in Villagio Arabo where he made laundry soap, but I never saw the local product; I bought our family's soap and detergent at the Yemeni alimentari.

A number of enterprising women kept chickens and a cow and sold eggs and milk from family to family. Other women came into the city selling camels' milk in the various small markets. I bought cow's milk from a woman who came daily to my door. At first, she brought the milk in a wooden container that gave the milk an odd taste we did not like in our tea or for the yogurt I made each morning. The taste may have come from smoking the container to keep it free of insects and Somalis had come to like the taste, as Europeans like their strong, stinky cheeses. I gave the woman a glass bottle for our milk and she usually, not always but usually, remembered to use it for my family.

Pastoral nomads came in from the bush, bringing goats and cows and a few camels to the Bakara market, a bare open area above and behind the city, behind where I lived. Italians preferred beef; most other families ate goat. Our family liked goat for our curries. Being used to aged beef, I had some trouble figuring out how to cook freshly butchered beef. Camel meat, a stable in the bush, was not as favored by city people. Slaughtering of livestock was done at the ocean shore and meat was sold in open markets in the city, plus in one proper glass-fronted butcher shop owned by a Somali from Nairobi.

Transportation in Mogadiscio was uncomplicated; Somalis walked from place to place. The municipality still managed a colonial era bus system; boys from the Indian community told me they used it. Three-wheeled motor rickshaws served all the neighborhoods. Fiat 1100 taxis running as jitneys along the main roads were a step up in comfort. Italians imported motor scooters, the Vespa, but they were sold mostly to foreigners. Bicycles were few and used mainly by children and the occasional servant because, as several Somalis told me, riding a bike makes one look undignified. They declared that a Somali prefers to walk or ride in an automobile, preferably a Mercedes-Benz. One man spoke wryly of the small, select group of Somalis driving expensive cars as a new tribe, the Wa-Benzi. Foreigners came with their own automobiles.

Televisions, VCRs, the popular juicer and other electrical gadgets would become available in the 1980s, but that was still in the future. In the 1960s electricity for Mogadiscio was expensively produced by diesel fueled generators, so even relatively prosperous Somalis could afford electricity in their houses, if at all, only for lighting.

One modern consumer item being sold in Mogadiscio and shops throughout Somalia in the early 1960s immediately caught the imagination of Somalis and was purchased by any man who could possibly afford it, be he pastoral nomad in the bush, farmer in a remote village or city dweller. It was the battery operated short-wave radio. One of our friends was known as Hassan Wireless because he owned a short-wave radio first, before anyone else. For Somalis, following the news from everywhere was a passion. Men gathered around a radio to hear news and talk programs on BBC and Radio Mogadiscio. A station from Saudi Arabia broadcast readings from the Koran in beautiful Arabic, a gift for Somalis like my gift of growing up with the wondrous English of the King James Version of the Bible. During the afternoon, radios in the bars and cafés, and in our home, stayed tuned into Radio Mogadiscio to enjoy Somali music.

Foreigners were targeted as customers for souvenirs. Boys hawked oddities such as pretty but uncured gazelle hides or objects carved from meerschaum, asking whatever price came to mind, and the foreigners paid, until they learned better. I regret not having bought gorgeous seashells boys were peddling to people in the beachclubs. A young man almost succeeded in selling me, for an outrageous sum, a bizarre carved multi-pieced wooden contrivance that took my fancy simply because it was so outlandish. To please me, Raj offered a reasonable price for it, but the fellow would not bargain. When we did not buy, he stayed on for a while and chatted with us. He was not desperate to make the sale. Gaining money beyond that necessary for the current standard of living was a game, as it is for speculators everywhere. The amount of money won was the way to keep score.

Older and more highly placed Somali men, like Omar Hussein, played a grander game of entrepreneurship. With borrowed money or with sums advanced from the foreigners, they bought land; constructed buildings they rented to foreigners; contracted with foreigners to provide them with workers such as servants, cooks, guards and drivers. They used their unexpected good fortune to live well and to support their fellow clansmen in Mogadiscio or in the home territory far from the city.

Evidently, Omar Hussein never had a second thought about refusing to lower the rent for us to the Indian price. He could afford to wait. He could live comfortably, fulfill responsibilities to his clan and even go on the Haj, the Muslim pilgrimage to Mecca, without income from his two-house compound. He could painlessly stand on principle as he understood it. The pale-skinned foreigner must pay the highest price. Other outsiders, lower on his prestige scale, would pay less, an amount appropriate to their lower status, and he accepted that. It reflected his good character and magnanimity.

None of the foreigners Raj and I knew in Mogadiscio ever mentioned to me the local pricing system for housing. Most likely, they were unaware of it because their embassy or employing agency contracted for their housing and paid the rent for them.

Throughout that year in Mogadiscio, I occasionally caught a glimpse of our almost landlord. Each time I saw him, he seemed a little heavier than before. In a shop on Via Roma a friend once pointed out Omar Hussein's wife to me. Instead of the garessa, the wrapped dress of cotton cloth worn by most Somali women, she wore the urban style long dress and flaunted gold earrings, a gold necklace and gold bangles. By our sixth month in Mogadiscio, Omar was wearing shoes and, instead of the hosgunti, trousers that looked as if made by a tailor on Via Roma rather than in Hamar Wein.

The Somalis I knew held Omar Hussein in high regard, for both his business success and his traditional ways. In addition to his urban investments, he was buying camels and paying kinsmen to keep the herd in his lineage's land in the north. It was well known that he helped a man in his lineage purchase a large number of camels, the required bridewealth given to the girl's family, so the man could marry. When his uncle died, Omar paid for food and drink at the mourning ceremony. He regularly hosted all night gatherings for his kinsmen where they chewed qat and told stories. He lent money to younger men, creating a network of admirers eager to please him and join his entourage. He prayed five times a day and, of course, attended mosque every Friday.

One afternoon, a few days before our year in Somalia was coming to an end, Raj and I met two friends in the Croce del Sud café for a drink. One was born and raised in Mogadiscio and the other, a member of the National Assembly, was from the north. I noticed Omar sitting at a nearby table, engaged in conversation with several men, three of them well-known political figures whom Raj had interviewed. They were all from the north, from pastoral nomadic clans. Raj exchanged greetings with them.

I remarked to our companions, "Omar Hussein is looking prosperous these days."

"He's a big trader now. He just returned from Rome. He was arranging a hunting expedition for a group of Italians. They like to shoot our leopards and take the skins home. For coats or something. He stopped over in Cairo and bought a lot of henna. Since he doesn't pay import taxes, he makes a nice profit selling it in Mogadiscio."

I was appalled. "It's illegal to kill the Somali leopard! There aren't many left. I caught one in my headlights when I was driving at night outside the city. It was absolutely beautiful!"

Our companions ignored my reaction. They probably considered it just one more amusing sign of female sentimentality.

Raj asked, "How does he get out of paying import duties?"

The politician said, "Think of the biggest name you know in recent appointments to the Ministry of Foreign Affairs. If you haven't heard the talk, you must have read about it in the newspaper. That is Omar's father's brother. Besides, now Omar can get Letters of Credit, so he withdraws foreign money from the bank at the official rate and sells it on the black market for Somali Shillings. A profitable business."

Raj said, "It's a dirty business."

Our companions looked at him in surprise. "Dirty? Why do you say that?"

"Because what he's doing is totally illegal. It is wrong."

They smiled and one said, "Oh, we thought you meant he was doing dirty work. Getting his hands dirty or working on construction. You know a northerner would never do that. But, what's wrong with his uncle helping him? The uncle has the position now and can do what he likes with it. Isn't that normal? Of course he will help people from his sub-clan. He's clever at doing trade, and he gives back part of the money to his uncle. Isn't that the right thing to do? They're good men. They take care of their own people. I hear he's looking around for a truck to buy."

I changed the subject. This would be the last conversation with our friends before leaving Mogadiscio. It would be useless to argue about good government or the proper functioning of an economy. The Somalis were abiding by rules in their own culture, plus the governmental practices they had observed Italians following before independence.

As Raj and I were leaving the café and passing by Omar Hussein's table he glanced up and obviously did not remember me. I did not bother bidding him farewell.

Now, in London's Southall, Omar Hussein still did not remember me. I was simply one more white woman, like so many others.

He asked, "How do you know my name?"

"I saw you once in Mogadiscio. I knew your father's brother. He was a big man. Everyone knew him." This was not exactly a lie.

I heard Raj call me. He and Kamla were walking toward us. Omar Hussein, suddenly excited, said. "Your husband is

152

Indian! Do you think he knows a place I can rent here for my wife and me? I cannot find an apartment. I asked three Indians already but they do not like dealing with an African. One would have rented to us but he was asking more than I can pay. I know for a fact it was much more than he charges Indians. "

When I introduced Raj and Omar Hussein, I could see from Raj's expression that he was trying to recall where he had seen this man before. I asked Omar to repeat his request and comments.

Raj started and quickly recovered, suppressing a smile. "Honestly, I can't help you. We are not from here. But good luck. Please excuse us. We have to hurry now."

I said good-bye and wished Omar Hussein good luck. I think I meant it, but a word came to mind as we drove away. It was a word from yet another culture and one I rarely used: *schadenfreude*.

OBSERVATIONS ON FEMALE CIRCUMCISION IN SOMALIA

During the entire two years I lived in Mogadiscio, being friends with Somalis and deeply involved in projects with Somalis, I rarely heard about or often thought about the Somali custom that later became a major concern of feminists and anyone concerned with women's rights: female circumcision. I heard stories I would later recall, but mostly I avoided the subject; it was too painful to think about. And I would have continued avoiding it if a young Somali friend (I'll call her Ruqyah) had not decided that she needed to talk about female circumcision and I should be her confidante.

It happened some ten years after I had left Mogadiscio, in the late 1970s, in Paris, where Ruqyah and I both were living. She described for me a reality little known at that time to anyone outside Somali society. As I listened, appalled by the very thought of female circumcision, I struggled to understand Ruqyah's situation but also to understand why Somalis, or people in any society, would inflict such injury on their daughters.

Why is female circumcision practiced? The Somalis I knew were not cruel. Most were very nice and some were exceptionally kind and responsible individuals. Nevertheless, obviously, they and their families practiced what I consider sanctioned brutality, and from all I knew, they never questioned it.

Ruqyah's need to talk with someone was precipitated when an older sister was visiting in Paris from Mogadiscio and had gone to a French gynecologist. Ruqyah accompanied her as interpreter. She said the doctor looked shocked when he saw what had been done to her sister and the nurse was close to tears. She told me that many Somali women are always in pain. Those who travel to a European country often seek medical care and for some things the doctors can help. They can make a better opening for urination. They prescribe antibiotics for infections. The doctor can ease the pain of cutting through scar tissue at marriage and first birth and can prevent tearing. Ruqyah said, with a note of desperation in her voice, that some women insist upon being sewn up again to heighten the husband's sexual pleasure.

Ruqyah was in love with a young Frenchman who wanted to marry her but all her women kinfolk told her that since she was circumcised she would have to return to Somalia to marry, that she was meant only for a Somali man. She feared the reaction of a French lover when he saw what had happened to her.

I was incredulous. It never occurred to me that this lovely girl would have been cut. In all respects, Ruqyah was different from most Somali women. She was far better educated than nearly all other Somalis -- men, women or children. She was born into a pastoral nomadic family in northern Somalia, where men herded camels and women kept the sheep and goats, but in 1961, soon after independence, and when she was still a baby, her family moved south to Mogadiscio, the new country's capital. Unlike her older sisters, Ruqyah knew only city life. Nevertheless, she told me, soon after her seventh birthday her Mother and a sister took her to what they called home, up north. She said they romanticized life in the bush. They thought of it as the good life. She found it a terribly backward place. Nothing but scrub grass and acacia trees.

She said, "Life is so hard for the family there. They are lucky just to get enough to eat. And the kids don't go to school. You can't have schools when people are moving all the time to find grass and water. I saw a big scar on a man's back and he said it was from a hot iron put there when he was sick. Something about letting out bad spirits. Was that supposed to cure him? Women die from infections after having a baby. No doctors. No hospital. Besides, I don't like living out in the open, the way they do. As for sleeping in that little hut ...

The women spend half their time putting it up and taking it down and it still isn't like having a real home."

Ruqyah said that when she was in the north she sensed the difference between her kinsmen there and people in Mogadiscio. Men in the north carried spears, later rifles and, eventually, machine guns. They were always ready to fight, at times to protect their camels from being raided or to themselves go raiding another lineage's livestock. Fighting between men from different lineages or subclans could become a vendetta and continue until a clan court was called to settle issues of justice and stop the killing.

The northern Somalis with whom I was friendly had long since left the pastoral nomadic life for city living. I knew them as men and women with a gift for language, as individuals who engaged enthusiastically in analysis and argument. In that era before television, conversation was our main entertainment. From them I heard stories about life in the bush. They said Somali children learned to be strong, to tolerate pain and accept it without complaining. An anthropologist friend told me, as did Ruqyah, of frequent conflict being built into the culture. If a Somali were wounded he should carry on as if nothing had happened to him. I heard that a doctor, in an extreme emergency, had to amputate a Somali man's leg without using an anesthetic and the man showed no sign of pain.

Ruqyah said, "I was not like the kids in the north. They are tough. They have to be. Well, Mother took me north and ... they cut me. They mutilated me. I thought I was going to die, I bled so much. Why do the old women do this to girls? Why do they want us to suffer? And to suffer all our lives.

"My mother and her sisters, and my sisters, tell me that female circumcision makes us halal, like a good Muslim. As if normal genitals are somehow disgusting or maybe scary. They think men and women both should be circumcised. Do you think that's true? My Turkish and Pakistani girlfriends never heard

157

of girls being circumcised. They think it's barbaric, and they are just as Muslim as we are. My sisters say we will never give up our Somali customs. Never. They say our mother did this for them and me and that makes us good Somali women. They say I shouldn't even think of marrying a foreigner."

I wonder if the view still holds today among Somalis that being circumcised, for both men and women, is basic to Somali identity. The concept of *halal*, meaning religiously sanctioned, ritually clean (not germ or dirt clean) is part of many cultures. Haram means ritually unclean. I know of no European language with such words. Before learning from Raj the Hindi word for ritually unclean, the closest in my experience to the concept of ritually clean/unclean was the Jewish *kosher*.

In Mogadiscio in the 1960s I did not hear the *halal* explanation. In fact, none of the Somali women I knew ever spoke with me about being circumcised. It was from men talking with my husband that I first heard about female circumcision. They told him, for example, about a prostitute who saved money so she could return to her family in the bush, be sewn up and marry as if she were a virgin. It was all very crude and scary and I didn't want to hear about it. The American anthropologist in Mogadiscio with whom I spent so many hours talking about Somali culture once, and only once, mentioned female circumcision to me. In those days anthropologists did not pay much attention to the woman's side of a culture. He called it infibulation.

As a woman and an anthropologist I felt I had to understand this bizarre practice. Why would deliberately damaging a daughter's body would be part of any society's culture? Why do they do this?

My anthropologist friend thought of female circumcision as a sort of chastity belt that reduces a woman's sexual appetite. He said Somalis think it has to be done because women are weak and will give in to temptation if their sexual desires are not curbed. Written commentaries on female circumcision, besides expressing horror over the practice, usually emphasize that it is practiced predominantly in patriarchal societies and is justified within the society as necessary for repressing female sexuality. Women are thought to be promiscuous if not circumcised. The *halal* explanation is often added.

One Somali friend, in telling my husband one of his many stories about Somali life, claimed that girls are circumcised because boys are circumcised and if the boy is losing something precious, so must the girl.

And it does appear that cutting girls is geographically related to male circumcision; it is found in societies along with male circumcision, but obviously, in no measure is it as widely practiced as male circumcision. We can wonder about the origins of male circumcision. A painting from five thousand years ago on the wall of an Egyptian tomb shows boys being cut. Herodotus, the first historian, 5th century BCE, a Greek from Halicarnassus (today's Bodrum, Turkey), reported male circumcision in Egypt, Ethiopia, and the Semitic Phoenicia.

Until fairly recent historical times, male circumcision was customary in very few societies outside this region of the world. It was not practiced anywhere in Europe or in most of Asia, Africa and the Americas. It spread as a cultural practice across the globe with the spread of Islam, beginning in the 600s CE. Male circumcision is in the Koran. Female circumcision is not and some scholars doubt the authenticity of its mention in the Hadith. In all branches of Islamic law male circumcision is obligatory, but in the major interpretations of Islamic law female circumcision is "noble" but not obligatory. It should be noted that in Islamic law female circumcision means cutting only the outer portion of the clitoris. The two extreme types of cutting are not sanctioned at all.

Male circumcision is more than the cutting of flesh from the penis. In most societies where it is practiced circumcision is ritualized in a rite of passage, a transition from one stage of life into another. (Contemporary neonatal circumcising of boys in the hospital and circumcision for medical reasons are separate matters.) In Jewish society the ceremonial cutting takes place eight days after the infant's birth. In certain African tribal societies the ritual initiates a boy into the warrior age grade. In Islamic communities the age at which a boy is circumcised varies. In some societies it is done as a religious rite before five years old and in others at adolescence and is accompanied by an elaborate public ceremony to celebrate the boy becoming a man. Circumcision also serves as source of cultural identity. In India, for example, circumcision is practiced by Muslims and marks them as a community separate from the Hindus.

Female circumcision is practiced today in Egypt, along the Nile and the rift valley into Sudan and down into Uganda and Kenya, the Horn of Africa, across the Sahel to Senegal in West Africa, among some of the Bedouins (pastoral nomads) of Saudi Arabia and Jordan; in the Kurdish mountainous country of Iraq and Syria; and in Yemen. In Indonesia, female circumcision, if practiced at all, meant a light, symbolic scrapping or snipping of the infant girl's clitoris, but recently a fundamentalist Islam has been introduced into Indonesia and with it the definition of circumcision as cutting the clitoris.

Ritual activity around the girl's cutting indicates that in societies that practice female circumcision it functions, like male circumcision, as a rite of passage from childhood into adulthood. Once in Mogadiscio I was invited to a women's party and discovered it was the celebration for a girl's cutting to be done the following day. The child sat in the back of the room, virtually unnoticed, while the women sang and one played a drum. They placed me on a large chair as if I were a man, and a woman danced a parody of a belly dance for me, as if to seduce me. Everyone, except for the girl, was laughing and having fun. The memory of the party remained in the back of my mind for decades, isolated from my other memories of Mogadiscio.

As I thought about male circumcision I could understand, reluctantly, why it has continued into the modern world but found no rationale whatsoever for the practice of female circumcision. The justifications given make no sense. Maybe some men everywhere fear female sexuality, but in most societies they do not respond by brutalizing their daughters. Ritual cleanliness, halal, has been achieved through less drastic actions. Other, more humane, rites of passage to ready a girl for her adult roles are used in other cultures.

As I listened to Ruqyah and continued puzzling over the why of this extreme practice a story told me by a Somali surfaced in my memory. It set my thinking along a different path.

One of my projects in Mogadisicio was teaching, along with two Somali men, in a primary school in Mogadiscio's casbah. One of my fellow teachers was sympathetic to my endless curiosity about Somali customs; I called him my cicerone and that amused him. He was from the casbah, a man of the city, and had little contact with Somalis from other regions of the country until 1960, the year Somalia became independent and the city expanded in size and complexity, especially with the influx of people from the pastoral nomadic clans, Somali's largest and dominant subculture. He told me of how customs differed from one Somali group to another, including differences in the severity with which a woman's genitalia is cut. (Sunnah circumcision is the removal of the prepuce, a retractable fold of skin or hood, and/or the tip of the clitoris. Clitoridectomy or excision is the removal of the entire clitoris and the removal of the adjacent labia. Infibulation is the removal of the clitoris, the adjacent labia minora and labia majora, and the joining of the scraped sides of the vulva across the vagina, leaving a small opening to allow for passage of urine and menstrual blood.) He said that his lineage, an urban community, did the least cutting and he would have his daughter circumcised in a hospital; that the most severe cutting was done by the pastoral nomads; that the village

161

farming people along the river practiced an intermediate level of severity.

My friend's narrative follows a pattern: in Somalia the harsher the life, the more severe the mutilation. For the pastoral nomads, food and water are scarce, their technology is simple, they live in isolated family-based groups. Drought can devastate the land and when rain does come it falls unevenly, capriciously over a lineage's territory. For the village farmers living along the rivers, nature is more under control, although not always benign. In the coastal cities, food, clothing, housing and some amenities were more abundant and available.

In brief, we observe people's response to the way they experience nature. Where nature is hard on people, people are hard on their bodies and on one another. Where nature is a bit more generous and their technology more advanced, people are a bit less harsh with themselves and with others. When people live more comfortably and securely in larger and more stable collectivities, they do not deliberately teach themselves to tolerate pain and are somewhat less inclined to inflict pain on others.

Female Genital Mutilation. When I first read this biologically accurate name for the ritual of female circumcision it reminded me of anthropological accounts of mutilation as a cultural practice found in societies around the world. In a number of 19th and early 20th century studies of small, non-literate societies anthropologists documented elaborate ritualized mutilation, mostly of boys. These societies were called primitive, but the people themselves were human beings and no different from people anywhere else; primitive refers to their level of technology and of societal complexity, not to the individuals within the society. They used stone and wood tools and lived in family based bands of some thirty individuals. The mutilation they practiced was usually part of a rite of passage into adulthood or a means of gaining spiritual power.

The Australian Aborigines, for example, a stone-age people, lived in small kin groups spread out across the hot, arid sub-continent. They circumcised their boys in a way not found elsewhere; they practiced subincision. In the coming-of-age ritual a boy had his penis cut through to the urethra, frequently leaving him with a lifetime of pain and sometimes with infection and bleeding that resulted in his death. In another initiation ritual the boy could have a front tooth knocked out or cicatrices cut on his body. For the hunting and gathering tribes on the Great Plains, such as the Cheyenne and Comanche, where life could have been as precarious as in Somalia, young men slipped leather thongs through strips of flesh cut in their shoulders and hung themselves by the thongs until they received a divine vision from the spirits. In contrast, the settled farming tribes of the Southwest, the Hopis, had no such customs of self-torture. They lived in a mild climate, grew food on irrigated land and stored it for winter. In their religious rituals, they showed a flair for artistic expression.

Ruqyah asked me, "Why do the old women do this to girls? My mother and aunts love me. Why would they want to hurt me?" She remembered her mother talking about her own circumcision, how she had endured it and survived, proving, she believed, that pain makes a woman strong. She and the other women felt they had to share this experience with their beloved daughters and thereby bring them into full Somali womanhood.

Imposing suffering from one generation to the next reminds me of hazing. Could that be a partial explanation of why women continue to cut their daughters? Hazing is done in many social groups. In the military, in fraternities, by sports teams. It verges on being a rite of passage. When a person enters a new stage of life or into a tightly closed organization, the people in charge assign him a set of ritualized unpleasant or difficult tasks. Once accepted into the group, the initiate inflicts these same nasty practices on new initiates. He and his compatriots survived, so why should the next generation not survive? The person wanting acceptance does as expected. He comes out on the other side with a new identity as a full-fledged member of the group. It is a transformation of the self. Moreover, a difficult initiation intensifies commitment to the social group and the group defends the justice of the hazing. Many people in societies with female circumcision defend the practice fiercely, as if questioning it were an attack on their very identity.

The answer to my question of why female circumcision exists is, essentially, that the cultural practice grew out of the mind's adaptation to an extraordinarily harsh natural environment and it continues as a custom embedded in ritual, as a source of cultural identity and who knows what psychological meaning.

I cannot say that this answer lends comfort to my feelings about female circumcision in today's Somalia and elsewhere. However, it follows logically from my understanding of female circumcision that people will move away from the practice when their life circumstances improve. Indeed, empirically, this is what has happened. Studies show that in countries today where female circumcision has been traditional the women who have gone to school or earn an income are less likely than other women to have been circumcised or to have their daughters circumcised. After a generation of urban living both men and women, especially the younger women, tend to stop demanding that their daughters and granddaughters be cut. The practice of female circumcision ends naturally as the community moves toward a lifestyle with greater stability and more creature comforts.

Of course, these abstract observations on the why of female circumcision tell us nothing practical about what can be done to protect girls from the present, real danger if their families want them cut. At the very least, in the case of immigrant families in the United States and in Europe or wherever girls are in danger of being subjected to the traditional practice, everything possible and wise should be done to rescue the girls and persuade the community to terminate the practice.

EPILOGUE

"It is not easy to speak about Somalia. The very nature of the country, the way of life of its people, and their cultural background, appear to evade objective thought and rational explanation. Most of those who have chosen Somalia as a subject for their scholarship have found themselves the inevitable victims of one of two emotions: they have either become enamoured with the Biblical character of the Somali way of life, the rich and the poetical language of the people, the absolute independence of the Somali in character, thought, behaviour and intellect, that at times may appear to outside observers as even bordering close to anarchism; or else they are overwhelmed with pity, by the harsh nature of the country's environment, the persistent fight of the Somali nomad against merciless odds, and his unawareness and even disdain for any association with modern technological advancements and amenities."

This was the introduction to a talk given in 1968 at The Royal Society of Arts by Mohamed Haji Ibrahim Egal, Prime Minister of Somalia. And I admit, having lived in Somalia when Mohamed Egal was Senator, before becoming Prime Minister, I was as amazed and impressed by the Somalis as were most other foreigners. But decades later, thinking back over Mogadiscio, I wondered -- Why would Somali men deliberately, consciously, and seemly without regret destroy their own beautiful capital city, deprive their people of a part of their history, and in the process destroy their government? What is it about their way of life, their culture, their independence of character? Somalia began with high promise. What happened?

It was my husband, Raj, who had chosen Somalia as the subject for his scholarship but without any special interest in the pastoral nomad's way of life or in the Somali character. He was a professor of political science and his interest lay in international law and government. He had done considerable library research on the United Nations' mandated establishment of Somalia's government, then applied for and received a grant to continue his research in the field, in Somalia. It was on this and another research grant that Raj and I and our two small children lived for nearly two years in Mogadiscio.

Raj was studying the process through which two quite different political and administrative systems, Italian and British, inherited from the colonial past were being shaped into a modern government for Somalia. I must admit that I did not follow his work closely. At home, while Raj researched Somalia and international affairs I was caring for our two children, carrying on a two-year anthropological fieldwork study of a Chicano community and teaching sociology in the university. When Raj announced that he had the grant, I saw to the children's schooling and health needs and made arrangements for our apartment and possessions while we were gone, then packed and prepared us for a long voyage to an unknown land. I had no time at all to read and reflect on the excellent anthropological studies then available of Somali pastoral nomads.

I went to Mogadiscio essentially as a wife and a mother but hoping for an opportunity to do field research. A few months after arriving, after the children were in school and comfortable with new friends, after setting up our home and getting used to the idea of needing a woman servant to help me keep house and a guard to watch over the compound, after seeing that Raj was fully engaged in his research, I looked to being an anthropologist and finding a community to study.

My study was of Hamar Wein, Mogadiscio's casbah, the original Mogadiscio, an ancient community with a fascinating history and culture. The rer Hamar were urban Somalis, city people who were different from Somali farmers in the inter-riverine area behind Mogadiscio and totally different from the dominant and most numerous Somalis, the pastoral nomads described by Mohamed Egal. The people of Hamar Wein called the pastoral nomads Rer Badiyo, People of the Desert, or more accurately, of the semi-desert. Sir Richard Francis Burton, on his extensive travels through northern Somalia in the 1850s, referred to the Somalis as Bedouin, noting that Somali nomads shared much of their way of life with the Arab Bedouin tribes.

As with the Bedouin, the central institution in the life of Somali pastoral nomads is, in anthropological terms, a patrilineal segmentary lineage system, a branching kinship system that determines much of how the nuclear family organizes its life vis-à-vis other groups in the society. It also places the individual in a particular relationship with family and kinfolk, a relationship very different from family and kinship in American and European cultures. In Somalia of the 1960s, the person remained throughout life identified with his/her family and kin groups, responsible to them, and they, in turn, remained responsible for him/her. If, for example, one man harmed another, the victim's family held the family of other man responsible and demanded recompense from the family, not from the person who had done the deed. Or, if a man gained wealth or a position in an organization, custom decreed that he use it to benefit his kinfolk as well as himself.

In the segmentary kinship system, the nuclear family belonged to a lineage, sub-clan, clan and clan-family. A man knew his ancestors at each level of kinship from the lineage upwards to his clan-family and, finally, to the Prophet Mohammed. In conflict (and conflict was common), a kin group stood together against more distant kin: brothers ally against cousins, cousins against second cousins, etc. in shifting coalitions depending on particular circumstances and interests. The clan-family stood at the highest and most inclusive level of the kinship system: the Dir, Isaaq, Darood and Hawiya, each with its clans, each clan with sub-clans and each sub-clan with lineages. The clan possessed traditional, historical rights over a large territory, over their part of the land that became Somalia.

Another clan-family, the Rahanweyn, a third of the Somali population and its most productive sector, were village-farming people in the south, living along and between two rivers, speaking a different dialect, almost a different language, from the pastoral nomadic clans. Any thorough description of Somali society will note that the farming people were at considerable social, economic and political disadvantage in the larger system dominated by the pastoral nomads.

Most of the Somalis I knew in Mogadiscio, other than people in Hamar Wein and the adolescent boys who liked to visit and talk, were Raj's friends, men in the government he met through his research. He knew the kinship system and kept track of who belonged to which clan and sub-clan because political parties were largely clan affiliated and represented the interests of the clan. He and his friends talked endlessly about political parties and political maneuvering in the National Assembly. A tale told in Mogadiscio was that if one went strolling at night and spotted a couple intensely involved, ignoring all around them, not to assume a romantic liaison; most likely it was two men arguing politics.

With Somalis conversation was continual, clever and usually well informed, including about events outside Somalia. They followed world affairs through BBC on short-wave radio, the local Italian language newspaper, imported newspapers, and scuttlebutt. I delighted in the back and forth of the talk, the argument, the verbal exchanges for the sheer pleasure of it. Language is the art form of a people whose material possessions are what they can carry in their hands or on the back of a camel. I have never encountered, before or since, so many individuals in one place who argued and analyzed so well.

I recall, vividly, one particular, most unlikely conversation. We were outside Mogadiscio, sitting on chairs around a table, furniture made in Hamar Wein by Indian carpenters, at a small stick-built, thatched roof restaurant, under an arbor of flowering orange and yellow bougainvillea, sipping sweet spiced tea served in glasses. Two urbane, highly placed Somali gentlemen had invited Raj and me to join them in a meeting with their rural clansmen. We had gone together in a Fiat 2000 along Somalia's grand highway, La Strada Imperiale, built decades before by the Italians and so potholed that we drove as often to the side of the road as on it. At the restaurant, five men, dressed in sarong, short-sleeved shirt and pillbox white cap had been waiting for us. The men spoke Italian, so as not to exclude Raj and me.

My vocabulary in Italian was not too bad, but having only recently picked up the language, I used it hesitantly and ungrammatically. I decided, nevertheless, after the business of the meeting had ended and the men were relaxing into casual conversation, to introduce a topic of my own. Raj's Italian was excellent, so I took a pen and notepad from my purse and wrote words for him to see and translate. A praying mantis landed on the pen and posed for me.

I asked the men to explain for me some ideas and practices in their religion. They were interested. I explained for them the words I would be using and gave them an outline, as I had done for students in my anthropology class, of Frazer's theory of magic and religion, describing the two types of magic and how magic differs from religion. They listened attentively. When I finished they applied Frazer's concepts to their own culture, systematically and in detail, separating out magical beliefs and practices from the truly religious. They were dead-on accurate. The men may have been literate in Arabic but probably not in Italian. Still, as I found often in discussions with Somalis, they were as skillful in expressing their ideas as were most of the formally educated people I knew.

Like these men, most Somalis had never attended a modern school. In the two decades leading to independence, the British and Italian ex-colonial administrations had established schools to educate a relatively small number of boys who would in time become an elite corps of professionals to take over the new government. The Somalis in Raj's and my social circle were young men, all of them fluent in English or Italian, who had once been among those privileged boys. I doubt that colonial administrators even considered schools for the children of rural nomads and farmers. Somali was unwritten. Somali secular and religious leaders could not agree on which of the possible Roman or Arabic alphabets to adopt, so children had no books in their own language to read. After independence, when the Somali elite could have decided otherwise, education was poorly funded and schools were city based, designed for sons of the elite.

A discussion of education in Somalia must take into account the duqsi, the centuries-old Koranic school where boys, and some girls, learned Arabic, religion and arithmetic, taught by a learned man, perhaps a sheik from the mosque. When walking about in Mogadiscio I occasionally saw men in gray robe and turban who were, I was informed in a tone of deep respect, from Al-Azhar University in Cairo and in Somalia to assist with the teaching of Arabic and Islam.

I observed two duqsis in Hamar Wein. Among the nomads the duqsi was held in the open under a tree or near a bush for shade but the ones I visited were both inside a building. I entered a large, airy room where straw mats covered the wood floor and children, some twenty boys and a few girls between six and eight years old, sat in rows, cross-legged, each cradling a wooden tablet. The boys wore clean but well-worn short pants and a shirt. The girls were in dresses. All were bare footed. A teacher sat in front of the classroom. At his side sat a somewhat older boy who acted as his assistant.

The children were learning the Arabic alphabet. They chanted in Somali the Arabic letters and a rhyme describing how to write the consonants and vowels "alif aa.. hoose, alif aa.. qor ... " Each wrote on his/her wooden tablet with a pointed stick dipped in ink made from crushed charcoal. At the end of the lesson they took their tablets to the ocean and washed them clean. The teacher explained that some of the boys were serious and continued studying with a teacher, as he had done, improving their literacy in Arabic and in reading the Koran. A chosen few apprenticed themselves to a Sheik in a mosque to learn the Koran and exegeses on the Surahs and the Hadith and, possibly, to become a sheik themselves.

I sat with the children and tried writing the letter alif, an A. I did not do it well and the children laughed at and with me. As I was leaving the classroom the teacher smiled and handed me the tablet I had used. It now leans against the wall among my plants in a sunroom.

I frequently heard foreigners in Mogadiscio say that Somalis are an intelligent people. The comment was made often enough that it set me to wondering why. The average Somali could have no greater natural ability than an average person anywhere else, but, indeed, Somalis were different. Compared to other new countries being established at that time, they were a small population, maybe two million, but the key difference was their economy: they were pastoral nomads, and for a pastoral nomad to grow and survive into adulthood in one of the world's harshest environments, in a society with a simple technology and no security other than family -- that requires an alert mind.

One resource only, a good-sized herd of camels, made life possible on the semi-arid Horn of Africa, and to manage it the nomad had to acquire a large body of knowledge, reason from it and act. He/she had to know, intimately, the flora and fauna of the land, the soil, the weather and especially when and where water was available. Rainfall in the area is erratic, wells few in number and not easily accessed, surface water uncertain and drought frequent. For maintaining the herd, the pastoralist had to be skilled in animal husbandry. He had to know every aspect of the animal, how to care for it, how to breed and increase the herd, how to manage it for milk and meat, for transport, to sell or use as a commodity. Equally, the nomad could not survive without knowledge of and deep commitment to the kinship system and culture that evolved with pastoralism. The nuclear family could not be economically independent. Usually they lived with a related family or two. As they moved across their territory in the never-ending search for water and grazing, they were continually making decisions, accommodating to a continually changing environment, planning for the seasons ahead but with contingency plans for the inevitable uncertainties. And for this they had to rely upon regular inputs of information only their kinsmen spread across the countryside could give them. They needed to share work with other kinsmen, meet for ceremonies, arrange marriages and settle disputes. The family needed allies but also often found competitors and antagonists they had to outwit and, sometimes, outfight. Having dealt with all this, the pastoral nomad believed he, or she, was the best and most clever person alive, capable of accomplishing anything. How else could he, or she, have survived?

During long periods of tending the animals, of little activity, of simply enduring, the Somalis had as a pastime their poetry and the play of language. A great man was famous as much for his oratory and the poems he composed as for his bravery and skill in battle.

This Somali combination of total self-confidence and readiness to learn and to act was impressive. An American who ran a program for teaching secretarial skills to Somali women described for me his first day of class. He had a room ready for the lessons, furnished with fifteen small table and chairs sets, each table holding an American typewriter. In the morning, when he opened the door, he found himself facing thirty girls, each wearing the traditional garessa, a dress formed from a carefully wrapped length of cotton cloth, and a small headscarf tied at the nape of the neck. These were his potential students, thirty proud, dignified young women, none of whom spoke English or Italian and were, therefore, since Somali was not yet written, illiterate as well, except, possibly, in Arabic learned in a duqsi.

The American asked, through his interpreter, "Can any of you type?"

Each and every girl answered, "Yes, of course, I can type."

He pointed to the nearest fifteen and said to them, "Please, sit down at a typewriter and show me."

The girls looked blankly at him, and one asked, "What is a typewriter?"

The teacher enrolled them all and proceeded to teach them, through the interpreter, to type English language text. Within weeks, every girl was typing, with fair accuracy, sixty words a minute.

U.N. specialists who trained boys in basic skills for government jobs such as surveying and census taking told me they had never before met people quite like the Somalis. I heard, for example, that the pastoral nomadic boys initially had problems with drawing; in their environment they had never seen a perfectly straight line. Showing up on time also had to be learned; for them, reading a clock and keeping an imposed schedule was an alien idea.

The unfamiliar or a lack of information did not humble a typical pastoral nomad. When I was teaching Indian boys in Hamar Wein I asked them what they wanted to be when they grew up. They answered, "I want to sit in my shop and work very hard." When the U.N. teacher asked the same question of the Somali boys they invariably answered, "President of Somalia."

President? Most likely the boys had little, if any idea, of what President meant other than it was the top position in a strange but impressive something called the government. They had grown up in a different economic and political reality. They had little or no experience with government and governmental services: police protection; roads; schools; postal system; water and sewage; electricity; assurance of access to food, shelter and health care, all that we take for granted. In their tribal society and economy, the bare necessities of life were provided, if at all, by family and lineage.

Somalis lacked government but they had a complex body of law and a legal system, all in a non-literate society. They had clan councils and courts. The social system was without inherited hierarchy or social classes; certain men clearly out-ranked the others, but essentially all were equal. High status was conferred by wealth, most often from selling livestock, and being from a prestigious lineage lent a certain advantage, but the qualities that earned highest respect were talent for rhetoric, strength in warfare, knowledge and wisdom. Men with these virtues led in the councils that met when they had need of deciding such matters as planning a war, making alliances with other lineages or sub-clans or clans or making peace between groups. To settle disputes such as murder, divorce, inheritance, theft or other matters of justice, they held courts. Pastoral nomads had no buildings; councils and courts were held in the open, in a place where men could conveniently assemble and practice their skills in political maneuvering.

I read that Somalis followed Sharia law, but no one in Mogadiscio mentioned it to me. A friend described for me a court, a shir, he remembered from his youth. He said that when men from different sub-clans or lineages were fighting and killing without end, in a vendetta, the lineages called on clan elders to set up a court to hear each side's version of the dispute and decide who was right and how many camels the guilty party should pay in compensation. He said laws were preserved in proverbs and in the memory of wise men. Even cases argued long ago were remembered and passed down from generation to generation, like judicial precedent. The old men told stories and children listened.

When a clan court was called the session began with one man introducing the case. The accusers and the accused chose men to represent them, men who were knowledgeable in the law and clever in debate. On the following day, when the court resumed, a man selected to do so recited the previous day's arguments and events, a feat of memory that would be usual in a society without writing, and argumentation continued until the elders were satisfied. Their decision on the case was enforced by respect for the law, by men assigned by the elders to enforce it or in battle.

The basics of Somalia's post-independence political system came alive for Raj and me when we accompanied a senator on a visit to one of his clan's villages. The village was unlike any farming community I have seen elsewhere but the political incident we observed felt familiar. We drove in a Land Rover across open scrubland to the village. Houses were low, round, stick-built with cone shaped thatched roofing. There was no modern infrastructure. We stopped at the edge of the village, parked the Land Rover and people came to meet us. We crossed an irrigation ditch and a man helped me jump it. A young mother, dressed in the garessa, followed along with us holding her infant for me to admire. The fields were cultivated with the hoe, which interested me because not too far from this land Ethiopian farmers used the plow, a far more effective tool for working the soil. I noticed broccoli and other unexpected vegetables growing in a small plot of land and a young man told me he had borrowed them from a U.N. experimental farm. For the large fields along the riverbank a strong rope strung between low poles stopped hippopotamus from coming on the land at night to forage.

As we approached the village center a line of men dressed in the usual sarong, some wearing a shirt and most bare-footed, came dancing toward the senator. Several were flourishing a spear. They were singing. Translation of the men's song: "One day we heard a great roar outside the village. We believed it was the sound of large machines coming to our village to build the paved road you promised us when you campaigned for our votes. We rushed out to greet the machines but alas, all we saw and heard were airplanes flying overhead." As he replied to their song, the senator was laughing. He promised that in the next National Assembly meeting he would double his efforts on their behalf.

A senator campaigned among his rural clansmen; they were his constituents. He had no others. Somalia's parliamentary system was a modified European form of government being grafted onto a tribal society. The Somali senator's constituency did not include social or economic classes; a class system across the country had not yet developed. He had no interest groups to represent; very few Somalis earned their living as professionals and civil society associations did not exist. Nor did the senator have businessmen as constituents. Most businesses were owned by Indians, Arabs, Italians and other non-Somalis, and continuing a practice from the colonial past, they were represented in government by a council of men from their own communities, not in the National Assembly by a senator.

During the years Raj and I lived in Mogadiscio the government was lead by a group of highly respected and, indeed, impressive men who had worked together in the period preceding independence to represent all the clans and to bridge the cultural differences between the northern clans and those of the south, differences exacerbated by the history of Italian colonials in the south and British administration in the north. The Somali founding fathers established a political party that continued, although challenged by smaller clan-based parties, as the nation's leading party. They were strongly committed to national unity over clan, but in a democracy all politics are local and local in Somalia meant the sub-clan and clan. Traditional leadership roles, the chiefs and sultans, were based within the kinship system.

Somali is an identity, not a nation. Nation means a people who share a culture and common interests that set them apart from other people and leads them to a shared loyalty and willingness to work and provide for the common good. From my admittedly amateur observations, the Somali pastoral nomadic social institution that functions similarly to nation is the clan-family: the Isaaq (Somaliland), Darood (Puntland) and Hawiye (southern Somalia where most of the armed conflict persists). Somali society has no institution above the clan-family, no royal lineage, as in European history, that symbolizes all Somalis and from which the institutions of a nation-state could evolve.

Religion did not unify Somalis as a nation. Sunni Islam gave Somalis a broadly defined common identity but it did not provide any organizational structure. A mosque was open to all believers but essentially belonged to the local community. The attempt to use religion for political ends was still in the future.

One political issue, however, did unify Somalis in their public life. Beginning with the independence movement, pastoral nomadic Somalis throughout the Horn of Africa were committed to expanding the borders of the Somali Republic to include three geographical areas that lay outside the Republic's initial borders -- land in Ethiopia, Kenya and Djibouti. Somalis were living in each of these areas, and in at least one they were the dominant tribe. The flag of the Somali Republic carries a white star with five points that represent the five lands of the Greater Somalia: north Somalia and south Somalia, already inside the Republic; Djibouti to the far northwest, formerly a French colony; the Ogaden at the northwest border, a region now in Ethiopia; and Kenya's Northwest Frontier District at the southwest border.

The expressed wishes of Somalis in Djibouti, the Ogaden and the NFD to join the Somali Republic were undermined or ignored by the colonial powers. Through political maneuvering, Djibouti remained French. The Ogaden and NFD had been colonial territories under the British. In both of these vast semi-arid grassland regions where nomads moved continually in search of land for grazing, frontiers between countries were far from precise, but in a final drawing of international borders, rather than support Somalia and the

Somalis, the British settled in favor of Ethiopia for the Ogaden and of Kenya for the NFD.

After independence in 1960, armed conflict and skirmishes at Somalia's borders with Kenya and Ethiopia continued unabated. As a consequence, the Somali government looked to building an army large enough to protect Somalis and to continue pressing its irredentist claims for the Horn of Africa, for the Greater Somalia. When the United States decided that a much smaller army was sufficient and needed for internal security only, the Somali government turned to the Soviet Union. During the 1960s, Moscow provided Somalia with full military equipment, plus Soviet military advisers and training in Russia.

As we later learned, Russia and China also provided Somali intellectuals with an ideological rationale for imposing a new political system to unify the Somalis as a nation.

If today's concepts of governance had been in the vocabulary of the 1960s all of us would have given greater attention to the government bureaucracies being built at that time. At the core of modern governments are bureaucracies run by career civil servants. In Somalia, under United Nations directives, British and Italian post-colonials educated a Somali elite for running the government but I wonder how the Somalis perceived the civil service. U.N. functionaries, men with whom most Somalis could not identity, were establishing the bureaucracies. What would have been a young Somali's level of intellectual and emotional engagement in the work? A friend, a U.N. official assigned to help set up one of the Ministries, spoke privately to Raj and me about the young Somali men he was training. He did not know how to motivate them. They did not show up for work on time, or even for days at a time; they had no interest in the work. For his young trainees the very concept of bureaucracy, with features such as hiring and promotion by performance and unrelated to kinship affiliation, would have been difficult for them to internalize.

At no time has Somalia survived without foreign economic aid, much of it to pay salaries and keep the government in place, but also in the 1960s for a wide variety of projects to build the economy. The U.N. locust control program was important. The U.N. Food & Agriculture Organization had projects to improve animal husbandry; experts worked with the pastoral nomads. Agricultural programs with farmers, earlier by Italians and after independence by the U.N., successfully increased and diversified southern Somalia's food supply, including bananas for export to Italy.

An anthropologist in Mogadiscio told me about a particularly promising project that could have provided jobs for the local people and become an export industry for Somalia. Taking into account the extraordinary fishing grounds off Somalia's northern coastline, a development assistance agency began setting up a canning factory for tuna fish that could be caught and brought to shore. However, the pastoral nomads in the area opposed the project and refused to work in the factory, even though an assured income would seem preferable to the difficult circumstances they coped with every day in their traditional economy. The project had to be dropped. The anthropologist had warned the agency, as would have Somalis if the foreigners had consulted them. Pastoral nomads considered themselves above doing menial labor, and besides, they could subsist well enough without this risky change to an unknown and low value lifestyle.

Other development programs set me to wondering what the foreign experts were thinking. In a particularly ill-conceived project the Russians brought huge tractors from Russia and plowed land outside Mogadiscio. Modern machinery produced an abundant first crop. After the second planting, a strong wind came, picked up the loose dry soil, turned it into dust and carried it away. No plant of any sort grew there again. Somali farmers understood their land but they had little or no voice in government.

Engineers told me about turnkey projects. Foreign experts designed and built the perfect machine or facility, then turned it over, with the key, to people who might not know why they needed it or, if needed, how it worked or, critical to its success, how to maintain it. Eventual failure of the project was inevitable but I heard no one question this modus operandi.

As I think back on discussions with Somali friends I recall no comments on and no analyses of the economy. Somali entrepreneurs in the modern economy were still new and few in number. In Somalia at independence, business and commerce were mostly foreign owned and economics had not been a major field of study for future leaders. The Somali leaders we knew were skilled in political matters; they understood how to organize; they were articulate, persuasive and knew intuitively how to size up people and disarm the competition. Many, maybe most, viewed their governmental positions and access to foreign aid primarily as means to gain income and fulfill obligations to their kinsmen.

Most Somalis were bringing pastoral nomadic modes of thinking and acting to the new government bureaucracy when what Somalia needed was people who understood hierarchy, respected authority, accepted supervision, would work in teams, invest their time and talent in doing a job with the expectation of promotion at a later time and without regard to clan identity, all for the good of the institution. For a pastoral nomad the culture of modern government was an alien culture.

A small personal incident illustrates the clash of cultures. A young man came to me, desperately seeking my help in saving his job as a driver with an American agency. He said he was being accused of cheating. He was puzzled and afraid. He told me he had done nothing wrong. I talked with his American boss. He said the young man was competent but would not follow rules about using the agency jeep. First he was caught using it to ride around with his buddies. He was warned but twice repeated the offence. It set a bad example and despite his general good performance the agency could not make exceptions. When I asked the young man why he broke an important agency rule he explained that the first time his cousins needed a ride and he felt he could not refuse them. The second and third times were even more difficult for him. He was on the road and passed by elders from his sub-clan. They would never understand his not helping them; it was his obligation to do so. Since their destinations were only a small distance out of his way, he took them in the jeep. He saw no harm in this. He said he was behaving normally, and his boss was wrong in not allowing a loyal assistant to give clansmen a ride in the jeep. I explained that his boss did not own the jeep; it was government property, public property, and not meant for private use. The explanation did not register with the young man. The agency kept him but after a while he left; his situation with them was untenable.

Modern civil service rules and clan-based cultural rules are conflicting value systems. Transition in any society from the tribal to the modern is neither simple nor automatic. Along the way it takes time, stability, experience and some reasonable accommodation to the existing culture.

I think it possible that if the Somali government of the 1960s had continued for another decade or two a generation of Somali bureaucrats would have acquired a professional identity as civil servants above and beyond clan. It could have been the institution to salvage Somalia's future. And the idea is not unimaginable; after all, the Mogadiscio police force, totally Somali, inherited from Italian colonial days and aided by the Americans, was led by responsible, impressive police professionals and it functioned well.

Raj and I and the children left Mogadiscio in June 1967, weeks before the National Assembly voted a new President into office. Pre-election debate had centered on Somalis in Ethiopia and their continual armed conflict with the Ethiopian army. The new President favored taking militant action against Ethiopia. He and his political allies had campaigned on securing the land across the border as Somali terrain, claiming it was land where Somalis pursued a pastoral nomadic life and therefore should be part of Somalia. In August, the President appointed Mohamed Egal as Prime Minister despite the fact that Egal did not agree with him about using arms for conflict resolution. Egal allied himself with politicians and administrators who were ready to focus on economic development rather than border warfare. To address Somalia's territorial claims, he used diplomacy and negotiation with Ethiopia and with other African countries,

In October 1969, the Somali army staged a coup d'etat, and hoping for an end to the existing rampant corruption and nepotism, many Somalis welcomed the new government. General Siad Barre arrested Mohamed Egal and other leaders. Determined to replace loyalty to the clan with loyalty to the state, Siad Barre installed his version of "scientific socialism," supported by the Soviet Union. He banned political parties, closed the National Assembly, abolished the Supreme Court, suspended the Constitution and selected himself as head of all the government -- the Supreme Revolutionary Council, the politburo, defense, security and the judiciary. Industries were nationalized and operated under his control. In a poorly conceptualized and eventually failed development program he had over a hundred thousand pastoralists moved from the drought-stricken north and resettled in the south. He instituted a number of needed reforms, including a literacy campaign, expansion of the school system and improved health care services, but the only positive action that lasted was his adoption of the Latin script for Somali.

During the mid-1970s, in a time of severe drought and star-vation, Siad Barre used scarce resources to build a large army in which he promoted men from his own clan. He had sought to eradicate tribalism but finally based his own power on alliances between his family's various sub-clans. He used a military unit composed of men from his sub-clan to inflict terror on everyone -- on others within his clan and clan-family, on the clan-family of northwest Somalia, and on clans in the south who formerly had been his allies. Corruption and cruelty characterized the regime. In 1991 his government was brought down by the union of two sub-clans who conquered Mogadiscio and then fought one another for control of what government was left and for ownership of the considerable humanitarian aid that was streaming into Somalia.

I began with quoting Mohamed Egal. He said in his address in London to The Royal Society of Arts in 1968 "... the absolute independence of the Somali in character, thought, behaviour and intellect at times may appear to outside observers as even bordering close to anarchism ..." In Somali society the threat of violence between men, lineages and sub-clans was ever-present but controlled and contained by custom, law and the clan courts. No such system of traditional law existed for resolving conflict between clan-families; there had been no need for it. Nomadic groups moved over a vast countryside; groups from different clan-families rarely, if ever, encountered one another; they barely even heard of one another. Then, in the mid-twentieth century, within a period of two decades, ex-colonial powers brought these Somalis together, expecting them to cooperate in a government modeled on European institutions for decision-making and conflict resolution, and they handed the government over, with money to finance it, to a small number of Somalis still rooted in a different and ancient world of rules and loyalties. The combination of clan based politics and access to foreign money and arms contributed to an unprecedented level of violence, and the disintegration of Somalia.

****

I lived in Mogadiscio for less than two years but that brief time changed the course of my life. I entered Mogadiscio seeing myself as an anthropologist and left realizing that research and teaching could not be my life's work. I was not certain what my eventual vocation would be but the search had begun and would continue as I moved from country to country as an expatriate wife, a woman following her husband and caring for their children as he pursued his career in an international organization.

Raj and I and the children arrived in Mogadiscio without any contacts at all in the city or in Somalia. Naturally, we checked in with the American Embassy but we were not part of the establishment. We relied on the local Indian men for information and advice about keeping house and living in the economy. Raj soon set up his research schedule, we enrolled the children in the Embassy primary school, and I went walking about in the city, chatting up anyone who would talk with me, observing and learning. I later heard that many Somali women assumed I was a doctor; the one other foreign woman they had known who dealt with them directly was an Italian pediatrician, long since departed but well remembered. On my first day in Hamar Wein, I was taken aback by a group of women surrounding me. An older woman held an infant and gestured that its mother had no breast milk. We stopped an Indian boy to translate for us. With trepidation, I said that in America babies are given cow's milk. They had tried that and it made the baby sick. I added that Americans boil the milk. The women talked among themselves and disappeared into the maze of narrow streets. I stood there feeling apprehensive: should I have said that? What should I have done? That same day I began teaching boys in a mosque and working with Somali teachers, both men; adjusting to this new and exotic world took me over. Yet, the plight of the women and the baby haunted me.

Months later, after I was more settled in, two particularly disturbing questions were thrust at me. They came from a young Somali woman who worked for my friend, Leyla, who lived in a compound near mine and whom I visited regularly. The young woman spoke Italian, as did Asha, the woman who worked for me. She and I exchanged pleasantries when I visited Leyla and when she stopped at my house to visit with Asha. One morning the young woman and I happened to meet on the road in front on my compound. I had just closed the compound gate behind me when I saw her. She was carrying a small child and two boys were walking beside her. I went to her, greeted her in Italian and asked the children's names.

Abruptly, she asked, as if she had been waiting for this opportunity, "Why do you have only two children? What will you do when they die?"

I did not answer. What could I say to her? Tell her that in my country children usually do not die and I could plan to have only two children?

She said, "I have lost two already. And this boy ..."

I reached out for her little one and she handed him to me. As he leaned listlessly against me, his small body seemed to weigh nothing. I said, "I will speak with Signora Leyla. She will have her doctor see your little boy. We will do what we can."

Realistically, as a foreigner who would soon leave the country, and as an academic, I could do nothing about Somali babies dying and nothing to lighten the burden of illness and untimely death patiently borne by everyone around me, especially the women. I loved teaching but would have preferred being able to help with Somalis' more immediate needs, those relating to matters of life and death.

Perhaps other women were also curious about my having two children, two years apart, but invariably we were speaking through a male interpreter, so they did not press the point, and I could hardly ask him to explain the why and how of my childbearing. At one of the many embassy receptions two young Sudanese women asked me, in halting English and almost whispering, how I managed to have only two children.

187

Since they seemed somewhat more prosperous than other non-European wives, I suggested we meet the following morning. I took them to the Italian pharmacy, and hoping the contraceptive pill was priced reasonably enough for them to buy, asked the clerk to show us the package. I explained the use of the pill. With the knowledge I possessed at that time, it was all I could do.

In the late 1970s Raj was with an international organization based in Paris and our children were in college. It was in Paris that I met Shugri, whose husband was with another international organization. She found it agreeable for us to be friends and spend time together; this was the third city and the second new language she was coping with since her husband had begun his new career and they had left Mogadiscio. With me she could speak English and talk about home. I found being with her agreeable and therapeutic as well. I had left Mogadiscio on my husband's schedule, not my own. For me, our stay in Mogadiscio had been far too short; at the time of our departure I was in the middle of my Hamar Wein ethnography and at the beginning of meeting women who particularly interested me for my research. Now, in Paris, I found a woman who would help me return, at least emotionally and intellectually, to complete something I had left unfinished.

Initially I tried to engage Shugri in exploring the history of Paris with me, especially in tracing the seven city walls, from the third century C.E. on the Ile de la Cité until well into the twentieth century. The thirteenth century wall of Philip Augustus was my favorite. Nothing about Paris appealed to Shugri's imagination. Neither did Mogadiscio interest her. She came from the north and a pastoral nomadic background and considered cities to be places one tolerates, not enjoys. We avoided any discussion of politics in Somalia or elsewhere. Instead, we talked for hours on end about our expatriate lives, the future she wanted and the future I wanted. Shugri had begun nursing school when her husband was stationed in

London, but they moved too soon for her to complete the program. She and I shared an intense interest in health care for women and children.

As with other expatriates in Paris, or any touristy locale, Shugri's apartment and mine were magnets for family and friends. We both had a steady stream of visitors staying with us. They came for vacation or they scheduled flights through Paris to spend a day or two, or more, with us. Visitors filled much of our time and reminded us of matters large and small we had left behind in our home countries.

Shugri's visitors were all Somali. A few had come to Paris for work in the embassy or in an international organization. Some came because they had finagled the trip from a governmental or international agency. Others could pay for the plane ticket with money they earned, probably from selling livestock on the hoof across the Gulf of Aden to Saudi Arabia or by dealing with foreigners in Mogadiscio, and they had decided to travel, knowing that on arrival at their destination family members who received them at the airport would take care of them.

For the people I met in Shugri's apartment, Paris was little more than an assemblage of buildings and pavement. They brought with them few images of the city's monuments, of its history, its romance. They had not read about Paris. Usually the men were literate, at least in Arabic. A number of the women had been taught to read with the new Somali script but books were not easily available. For them book meant the Koran. I doubt they had seen movies set in Paris. Most of the cinemas in Mogadiscio were intended for men only, but even if the women were going to the cinema, the films were more likely to have been made in Bombay than in Hollywood or Paris.

Shugri's guests were not far removed from the pastoral nomadic life, one totally dependent upon the herding of camels, with camel milk the basic food supplemented occasionally, especially at weddings and other ceremonies, by camel meat. Families moved from one camp place to the next, according to when and where the monsoon rains had fallen, or failed to fall, and where water could be brought up from deep wells. The land was dry, harsh and rock-strew but the acacia tree thrived and between rains gave cover to a wide variety of bushes and smaller trees that supported a rich variety of wild life. Camels foraged on bushes and any green plant available. Men kept the camels and, further south, cattle. Women raised goats and sheep. During the day older boys shepherded the camels and at night the family gathered all the animals into a thorn bush corral, keeping them safe from leopards, lions and hyenas.

In Mogadiscio, a Somali friend, Warsame, told me about being a twelve year old watching the family's herd. When out with the camels and milk was scarce they went hunting, usually for dik-dik, a small gazelle. (this in spite of my reading that pastoral nomads do not hunt animals for food) While the two older boys hunted, Warsame prepared a fire, in hope and anticipation. When the boys returned with their speared gazelle they quickly cut open the animal's belly, took out the liver, threw it on the fire for a brief moment before devouring it. Their hunger somewhat assuaged, they cut the carcass and roasted the meat.

Warsame's learning to be a pastoral nomad had begun even earlier, from games his mother played with him. Shugri did not use the games with her own children, but she had grown up with them. A few were familiar to me, such as a silly little thing with babies. I walk two fingers slowly up from the toes, saying, "here it comes, here it comes" and, as the child squirms in anticipation, walk faster and faster, to end suddenly with a "tickle, tickle" and much giggling. A Somali woman walks her fingers playfully the same way, beyond the tickle, up to the child's face and, using the thumb and middle finger, ends with a sharp rap to the tip of its nose. Pleasure is followed by a hurtful surprise and laughter from adults. In races and competitions between boys, the losers were taunted, made fun of and dared to cry or show resentment. Any physical or psychological defect could easily turn into a nickname, such as Lame (Zoppo) or Stutterer (Shig-Shigo), that the boy carried through life. (Siad Barre's nickname was Afwein, Big Mouth.) The games taught children traits indispensable to survival in the life ahead of them: endurance, stoicism, fierce defense of self, enjoying the pleasurable moment without regard to future pain.

Men seemed not to work, except at the well. They endured long treks with their camels and were always prepared to fight. Women did the usual endless women's work, plus at each campsite they built the family's sole residence, the aqal, a large and substantial hut. They formed its frame with branches shaped and saved for this purpose and covered these and the interior floor with fine, beautifully made grass mats they had woven. When father decided they must move on to seek fresh grazing land or for water, the aqal was quickly dismantled and loaded, along with their other meager belongings, on to the pack camels.

Cities were marginal in the pastoral nomadic life, places they entered only occasionally. Northern Somalia had Berbera, a port, regularly fluctuating between 15,000 and 30,000 inhabitants as nomads came and went, mostly to sell livestock. The only other towns were Burco and the larger Hargeisa, a transportation crossroads. The Ottomans once controlled Hargeisa; after 1941 it served as the British colonial capital.

The true urban centers that lived in the imagination of most Somalis were Mecca and Medina, destinations on the holy pilgrimage. Those were the cities Shugri's kinfolk had dreamed of visiting. Not Paris.

Shugri's visitors took a standard tour or two around Paris, but mostly they sat endless hours in her apartment, talking and telling stories. I enjoyed sitting with them, and she translated for me. As in Mogadiscio, I relished the back and forth, the story telling, the verbal exchanges for the sheer pleasure of it.

In Mogadiscio I had no friendships and far too few contacts with Somali women, largely because of the language barrier. Few Somali women spoke Italian or English. I had picked up Italian but little of the very difficult Somali. A number of young men served informally as my interpreters. I helped them improve their English, and they helped me carry on conversations with a wide variety of people, mostly men. Not one Somali man I knew would have sat with me and a group of women discussing women's work or, especially, patiently translating the questions I would have posed. It would have been beneath his dignity.

For some reason I had not become friends with the three very attractive bilingual Somali women I occasionally met in Mogadiscio and with whom I could speak directly. I do not know why I saw so little of them. Perhaps it was because they were engaged in activities with the American Embassy wives and I was not part of that social set. More likely it was because Raj focused on politics, both Somali and international, and I found myself caught up in Hamar Wein with matters dominated by the male side of society.

Raj and I, as part of Mogadiscio's social world of foreign experts, were regularly invited to official parties and diplomatic receptions, along with top Somali politicians and government officials. Many Somali men attended. They liked the talk, the food, the drinks. They were quite sophisticated, speaking English or Italian, well dressed, charming conversationalists. Wives rarely came with the men. They were country women speaking only Somali, wearing Somali dress. At first, when they did appear at such an event, I went to them and introduced myself, but without a language in common we felt too awkward to continue. Invariably, after being formally greeted by the hostess, the Somali wives clustered at the edge of the action. They had neither their husbands' bilingual facility nor experience with the international social set's entertaining etiquette. Most had never used a fork, knife and spoon; sipped tea from a china cup; balanced a cocktail glass, napkin and canapé while engaging in small talk. They looked uncomfortable in the unfamiliar setting, and I wondered what they thought of the houses their husbands now commanded, houses the colonialists had abandoned when they returned to Italy. No matter how authoritative and competent a traditional woman may have been in her own setting, attending a party or a sit-down dinner in the modern sector of Mogadiscio' society must have been agony for her.

I understood how the women felt; as a girl from the lower working class, I myself had gone through a sometimes-embarrassing period of learning middle-class social manners. I would have liked to help but did not know how to reach them. When, at last, a bright, pretty Somali girl in her late teens, fluent in English, offered to became my interpreter and ally in meeting and talking with the matriarchs behind the scenes I could do nothing other than mutter to myself in disappointment. The following week we would be leaving Somalia to return home.

By the time I met Shugri, I had discovered the work I wanted to do: the unfashionable, undervalued field of family planning and primary health care. I had lived in Turkey and India, followed by four years in the American Midwest while my children finished high school and went on to college and while Raj worked abroad with his international organization. During that time I returned to school and qualified for work in public health.

Now, in Paris, I found a Somali woman with whom I could talk and who shared my concerns. In her living room, through her, I belatedly made real contact with ordinary Somali women, her many cousins and aunts.

Shugri and I asked questions of the women. How many babies have you had? How many pregnancies? How many live births? How many miscarriages? How many of your babies died and how many grew up and married? Think now, and try to remember. Think about your mother, your older sisters, your older women cousins, your aunts, your grown daughters. How many babies did each of them have? Pregnancies? Miscarriages? How many of their children survived into adulthood? Shugri probed and we listened as the women remembered, shuddered over the pain, saddened at the memory of a beloved child now dead.

We calculated that, on the average, by the time she reached menopause (if she lived that long), a typical Somali pastoral nomadic woman had gone through twelve pregnancies, four miscarriages, eight live births and had seen four children survive into adulthood.

Had I been in these discussions with Shugri and the women in later years I would have been more skillful in asking different and additional questions. We did not, for example, linger over talk about death in pregnancy or childbirth and we certainly did not discuss the complications at birth and sometimes-deadly infections caused by female circumcision.

Later, I went into specialized libraries in Paris for information. The infant and child mortality rates Shugri and I found in our informal sample were typical of Somalia. The Somali maternal mortality rates of 1,600 per 100,000 live births were among the highest in the world. Life expectancy was 47 years.

I asked a Somali woman why women have so many children. She answered, "To keep her husband." A man had the right to as many wives as he liked and could afford. An older wife, she said, hopes that children will tie her husband down to his marriage with her. She reminded me of the high divorce rate among Somalis. For years, the number of divorces recorded in Mogadiscio equaled the number of marriages. A few young Somali men told me tales of childhood, of having to accept father's new amour, sometimes of mother and small children leaving while older brothers and sisters stayed behind. A woman did not change her lineage identity at marriage to join her husband's lineage; she retained the right to return to her family of origin with the younger children, but her children belonged to the father's lineage.

A practical reason for a woman having many children becomes obvious when considering the pastoral economy. Children were a mother's work force. She had full responsibility for her flock of sheep and goats, which provided for the family much of what they could not produce themselves. Their sale bought cloth for the family's clothing. A five-meter length of cotton cloth became a woman's dress. Men wrapped a length as a sarong and used another as a shawl. The animals also could be bartered for weapons, gold and silver jewelry, coffee beans, tea and other small luxuries.

From a World Bank study I learned a surprising fact never presented in discussions with anyone in Somalia: the value of sheep and goats exported to Saudi Arabia considerably exceeded the value of the men's camels and cattle that were exported. In other words, women were contributing, without it being acknowledged, more to national earnings than were the men. Women worked harder than men, contributed more than men to the economy, yet a woman was valued personally at half the value of a man, expressed by the fact that when a woman was killed, the responsible lineage paid her lineage only half the price in camels they paid when they killed a man. The injustice of it all infuriated me.

Children were expected to work. Caring for animals is labor intensive and a child can chase a stray lamb, tend the sheep, pull along the lead goat, bring branches from a thorn bush to build an enclosure, carry a water container. If she could find land with a natural depression where water had collected, the mother planted millet, then had children guard the crop against birds and other wild animals. Children may have been a mother's only security in old age. Even if convenient and reliable contraceptives were available, given the death rate for infants, a woman needed many children to ensure that at least two sons and a daughter or two survived.

The suffering Shugri's kinswomen so stoically recounted shook me, and given the potential for a population explosion built into our figures, I feared for Somalia's economic and political future. How could the Horn of Africa, with its grassland already degraded by livestock overgrazing and no known alternative resources, support a doubling of its population every generation? In the past, a high death rate from disease and illnesses was constant and periodically a society would be decimated by food shortages caused by drought, flood or insect invasion. Mostly the very young died first; a high birth rate countered a high death rate. However, in recent decades, even in remote societies, modern medicine has intervened. Access to better health care is increasingly available. The infant mortality rate drops; the number of infants per woman does not drop commensurately; the population grows. Somalis are among the people on earth who receive the fewest health care services and who are burdened the most with illnesses, yet their population growth rate is among the world's highest.

A population explosion did not worry Shugri. No matter how often I talked about family planning, however I presented my argument, the idea of many more Somalis appealed to her, but she was touched by the Somali woman's wretched state of health and the babies dying. I stressed the importance of family planning for women's and children's health, and she agreed with that. Even the man, the only man who sat in on our conversations, recognized that something had to be done. He had seen during his travels in Europe that death need not steal away a family's children. He did not mention the toll of multiple pregnancies and births on a woman's health, but he did wax enthusiastic about preserving the lives of a man's offspring.

Such a visit with Shugri and her family was the last time I saw her. I could not reach her to let her know I would be gone for a while. When I returned home two months later Shugri and Mussa, her husband, were no longer in Paris. One of Mussa's former colleagues thought they had left for London. I hope, for their safety, they had not returned to Siad Barre's Mogadiscio. In the late 1970s Mogadiscio was overwhelmed with refugees from fighting in the Ogaden, and Siad Barre's clan would at war with Shrugri and Mussa's clan.

I would have liked to tell Shugri my reason for leaving Paris so abruptly and then talk again with her when I returned. An international agency had called and asked me to leave within the week for Indonesia. I went as a consultant to evaluate a rural health care program for the Ministry of Health. I had at last entered into the world of work I loved, primary health care in developing countries. Shugri was the one person who would understand and care about how important Mogadiscio and Somali women had been in shaping this part of my life, and she was gone.

I would not see her or hear from her again. Such was the expatriate life.

About the Author

Iris Kapil grew up during the Great Depression in western Pennsylvania-eastern Ohio. She attended the University of Wisconsin-Madison, where she received a B.A. (1953), met and married a Fulbright Scholar from India, had two children, and received an M.A. (1962) in anthropology. They later adopted another child.

During the 1960s Iris taught sociology at the University of Wisconsin-Milwaukee and, with her husband and children, began living abroad. In Somalia, Turkey and India she conducted sociological research projects, from which she published academically.

In 1972 Iris returned to the U.S. for the children's schooling and her graduate studies at the University of Chicago. She transferred in 1973 to the Kellogg School at Northwestern University for an M.B.A. (1975) in Hospital/Health Services.

After a year with an American public health program Iris moved to Paris, France to be with her husband and for twenty years worked in the planning and evaluation of primary health care programs in Turkey, India, Indonesia and the United States. She now lives in the Research Triangle, North Carolina.

.

CPSIA information can be obtained at www.ICGtesting.com
Printed in the USA
BVOW030642210212

283385BV00002B/4/P